Millennials
INTO
Leadership

Millennials
INTO
Leadership

The Ultimate Guide for Gen Y's
Aspiring to Be Effective,
Respected, Young
Leaders at Work

LISA ORRELL

The Generation Relations Expert
Speaker · Author · Leadership & Career Coach for Millennials

Intelligent Women Publishing
A Wyatt-MacKenzie Imprint

Millennials Into Leadership
The Ultimate Guide for Gen Y's
Aspiring to Be Effective, Respected, Young Leaders at Work
by Lisa Orrell, CPC

F I R S T E D I T I O N
ISBN: 9781936214006

Library of Congress Control Number: 2009937854

Intelligent Women Publishing
A Wyatt-MacKenzie Imprint

Imprint information: www.WyMacPublishing.com

Printed in the United States of America

Dedication

This book is dedicated to the Millennials who are our current and future leaders – whom I believe will do right by all of us. It's also dedicated to my fab family: Adrienne, Jenner, Julie, Ma & Pa Jones, Mom, and Papa O.

Acknowledgments

I'd like to extend a special "Thanks!" to Debbie Feldstein, Principle of Creative Blocks Editorial Services in New York City (CreativeBlocks.com). Her assistance with research and content development were invaluable. You rock, girl!

And I'd also like to extend a heartfelt thank you to thought leaders and experts who generously provided content for my book: Linda Holroyd, Founder of FountainBlue.biz and creator of the *When She Speaks, Women in Leadership Series*; Millennial Dan Schawbel, personal branding expert, and author of *Me 2.0: Build a Powerful Brand to Achieve Career Success* (Kaplan, 2009); Millennial Ryan Healy, Co-founder of BrazenCareerist.com; and, the fabulous Sara Roberts, CEO & President of Roberts Golden Consulting, and co-author of the best-selling book, *Light Their Fire: Using Internal Marketing to Ignite Employee Performance and Wow Your Customers (Kaplan, 2006)*.

However, above all, my long time partner, Adrienne, deserves my biggest acknowledgment. I could easily go on and on expressing my gratitude for her endless patience, love and support. But, you didn't buy this book to read about that, so I'll simply say this to her: *THANK YOU!*

TABLE OF CONTENTS

❖

PART THREE
Key Components for Successfully Building & Retaining
Your Team

❖

PART FOUR
All About Lisa

What Experts Say About *Millennials Into Leadership*

"The single biggest challenge America faces over the next decade is managing the transition from a Boomer led country to one dominated and led by America's next great generation, Millennials. In this book, Lisa Orrell provides members of that generation their first practical 'how to' advice on succeeding in their new leadership roles. Hopefully, many Millennials will read this book, take her advice, and lead our country, and our companies, into their next era of excellence."

Morley Winograd
Co-author of the Bestselling Book: "Millennial Makeover: MySpace, YouTube
and the Future of American Politics"
www.millennialmakeover.com

"After speaking to thousands of college students nationally, and communicating with tons of professionals within corporate America and higher education, I truly believe that this 'powerful' leadership book written by Lisa Orrell will not only benefit the (current & aspiring) new Millennial leaders immensely at work, but it will help these emerging young leaders create a better nation and world!"

Joshua Fredenburg (Millennial)
National Leadership Speaker, Generation Y Expert, and TV Commentator
Author of: "A Call to Action; 14 Highly Effective Leadership Principles
for Leaders Of Millennials"
www.visionxy.com, www.generationyleadershipedge.com

"Lisa Orrell is a foremost authority on Millennials. She's been educating employers about you (us!) for years and now also focuses on energizing our young generation directly – to be the leaders we all know we can be. Lisa's information-packed *Millennials Into Leadership* will prompt you to read again and again for more nuggets of wisdom to excel your career."

Heather R. Huhman (Millennial)
Founder & President of Come Recommended
www.comerecommended.com

"Lisa Orrell has once again hit a home run in her latest book! Since leadership effectiveness is the single biggest differentiator in a successful career, reading this book is an absolute necessity for any young adult wanting to be a star in their field."

Rayona Sharpnack
Founder & CEO of Institute for Women's Leadership
Author of: "Trade Up: 5 Steps for Redesigning Your Leadership & Life from The Inside Out"
www.WomensLeadership.com

"*Millennials Into Leadership* is an essential and timely book for Millennials who have the ambition to make great things happen, but need a guide to help them reach their full potential as young leaders in the world and in the workforce!"

Dan Schawbel (Millennial)
Personal Branding Expert
Bestselling Author of: "Me 2.0"
http://personalbrandingblog.com

"The world is facing a crisis of leadership. Some of these problems threaten our very existence. Leadership is not a title on your business card! *It's a way of behaving.* Global business leadership is about solving global problems profitably. Don't wait until you're a Half-a-century old like me to step up and do your part! The world needs you now, and Lisa's book is a terrific guide to leading effectively as a young adult."

Kimberly Wiefling
Founder & President of Wiefling Consulting, LLC
Global Workforce Consultant & Author of: "Scrappy Project Management - The 12 Predictable and Avoidable Pitfalls Every Project Faces" (Also available in Japanese from Nikkei Business Press)
www.wiefling.com

"Lisa is one of the foremost experts on what Millennials can and should do to advance their careers beyond the internship and entry-level stage and into leadership. If you're a Millennial – or someone who cares about a Millennial – then this is the career book for you."

Steven Rothberg
Founder & President of CollegeRecruiter.com
www.CollegeRecruiter.com

"Want to see the future? Orrell's new book provides a fascinating advance preview of a crucially important future generation of leadership. She also will help shape this future with her many cogent and insightful suggestions to these young budding leaders. Orrell 'gets' this new generation, and any young person today with aspirations to leadership needs to study this important book carefully."

Jonathan Pontell
Social Commentator
CEO, The Pontell Group
www.JonathanPontell.com

"Regardless of person's age, or the size of the organization where they work, every person I've ever coached wants to have their talents used wisely. Millennials are no exception. By following Lisa's guidance, Millennials can be even more effective in making their contribution as young leaders, regardless of their current role, and get excited by the work they do."

Camille Smith
Founder & President of Work In Progress Coaching, Inc.
25-year Leadership & Executive Coach
www.WIPCoaching.com

"Enough already with your gripes about the Gen Y'ers! We can all avoid the tired old generational gap mistake and instead choose to learn about, and from, our new Millennial comrades. I bought copies of her first book, *Millennials Incorporated*, for my executive team, and then hired her to conduct seminars for us on several occasions. But her *new book* is going to be a must-read for the young students and young employees at our 110+ schools nationwide! Learning how to be an effective leader needs to start early, and Lisa's book provides Millennials with what they need to know. We old guys have a lot to share, but we can also learn a lot from, and support, this wonderful generation. Thanks, Lisa, for bringing us all together!"

Winn Claybaugh
Co-founder, Owner, and Dean of Paul Mitchell Schools
International Motivational Speaker & Author of: "Be Nice (Or Else!)"
www.BeNiceOrElse.com
www.PaulMitchellTheSchool.com

"Lisa's new book is the next in a line of excellent publications that are critical to read for understanding effective management and leadership principles. As a Millennial, I wish this book were available when I took on my first managerial role. It is an invaluable resource."

Richard Bottner (Millennial)
President of Intern Bridge, Inc.
Author of: "Total Internship Management – The Employer's Guide to Building the Ultimate Internship Program"
www.InternBridge.com

INTRODUCTION

Startling Factoids On Why This Topic Is Important...It's All About YOU So Don't Skip This Brief Intro!

Hello! And welcome to my book. I can't believe I'm sitting here writing another one so quickly after my first, but I felt this topic and focus was important. You probably didn't read my first book, *Millennials Incorporated: The Big Business of Recruiting, Managing and Retaining the World's New Generation of Young Professionals.* That's okay – I don't take it personally. After all, it was *about* YOU, so it was targeted at companies wanting to understand you as future/current employees, plus I included a lot of tips to help managers and supervisors engage with your generation more effectively.

So, I've been on your side for quite some time and helping employers figure you out...all in an effort to recruit and retain your generation as their future leaders. And, I've even conducted work-shops for Millennial employees to help them acclimate and ramp faster as new professionals in the workforce.

It has been a wild couple of years in my life focused on YOU! I've conducted many seminars, workshops and keynotes with audiences full of generations older than you...often watching them spend the first 15-minutes of the presentations looking at me with blank stares. But then, luckily, I see the light bulbs start to appear over their heads as they begin to "get" what I'm sharing about your generation. And then I also witness that look of "Uh-oh" from them as they realize they're going to have to really step-up their personal leadership and management game to better retain their Millennial employees.

Why? You guys demand a lot from your leaders at work! And, quite honestly, there are a lot of mediocre managers/leaders out there in the workforce, and your generation is requiring them to reassess their personal management and leadership skill set(s). Some of them haven't had to do this in a long time and they are struggling with it (and/or resent it). But, I think it's good for them. A little "reality check" for people who have "gotten by" on mediocrity is necessary to improve a company.

Why my new book? It's rather simple really. From a demographic standpoint, your generation will be moving into leadership roles sooner than many generations before you did. It's basic math: The Boomers are a massive generation and starting to hit retirement age now, and Gen X (the 30-somethings) are a small generation. And even though Generation Jones (the 40-50-somethings) is a pretty big generation, they're replacing many Boomers in senior management and leadership roles now. That means in the U.S. we don't have enough head count to fill the entry level to middle-management roles that are becoming available (there just aren't enough Gen Xers to do it).

Let me share some quick stats to put this in perspective…but it's NOT just a U.S. "labor shortage" issue:

1. According to the US Bureau of Statistics: By 2010, U.S. corporations, and small to medium-sized businesses (SMB's), *will be short 10 million workers.*

2. The EU's Labour-Shortage 'Time Bomb' (June 22, 2007): In the European Union, a shortage of 300,000 qualified employees in the IT sector *alone* is forecast for 2010.

3. 'Japan Stares Into an Economics Abyss', Masaki, H. (May 14, 2006): In Japan, prospects for skilled labor are so dim that some electronics manufacturers have introduced programs granting their employees leave (time off) to receive fertility treatments.

4. (U.S.) Employment Policy Foundation (EPF): A systematic labor shortage is expected to transform the workplace over the next 25 to 30 years as the gap between Baby Boomers and entrants of college-educated workers widens due to the Boomers' mass retirements. If the U.S. economy continues to grow at 3% a year – the economy's consistent average since 1948 – the workforce will have to increase by 58 million employees over the next three decades if the same rate of productivity is maintained. Yet, if the current population trend continues, the number of workers will only increase by 23 million. This trend would cause an overall *U.S. labor shortage of 35 million workers.* Most of these projected shortages are expected to involve workers having specific skills. *My comment: The first "wave" of this U.S. labor shortage was described in stat #1 on this list.*

Okay, those are just a *few* reasons "why" you may find yourself (or have already been) promoted into a management position and leading a team sooner than you expected (probably supervising some employees older than you are).

And while this is "good" news for your career growth, I personally provide one-on-one Leadership & Career Coaching for many Millennials (many of which hire me on their own – not through their employers) who are struggling. They have only been in the professional workforce a short time, maybe 2-5 years, but are finding themselves in positions with a lot of responsibility. So they don't have a lot of real-world leadership and management experience, let alone experience in their field, and they need help "ramping fast" as leaders within their companies.

So that's the goal of my book: To give you an overview of what being an effective leader means, help you understand the difference between a manager mindset and a leadership mindset, provide you with effective leadership tips, and help you achieve respect (and confidence) as a young leader at work.

I don't believe that old saying "leaders are born – not made". I work with many young professionals who are smart and talented, but need my help to grow quickly in a leadership role.

And one thing to note: Having a leadership mindset, regardless of your current position at work, or even if you're still in school, will do nothing but help you succeed now, and in the future. Highly successful executives, 2-3 times your age, never stop learning and continually embrace ways to improve their leadership skills. So get started NOW, and give yourself an edge…personally and professionally.

YOU are the future of the workforce (and our world!), and your co-workers, employees, supervisors, and *employers*, need you to be the best leader you can be…so let's get started!

Lisa Orrell, CPC
The Generation Relations Expert
Speaker • Author • Leadership & Career Coach For Millennials
www.TheOrrellGroup.com
Lisa@TheOrrellGroup.com
1-888-254-LISA

Check out Lisa's Busy Blog: Blog.GenerationRelations.com

Listen to Lisa's Popular Podcast:
MillennialsInMotion.podomatic.com

Follow Lisa on Twitter @GenerationsGuru

Join Lisa On: FaceBook, MySpace and LinkedIn

P A R T   O N E

Understanding Your Multigenerational Workforce

"63% of top executives say that most managers' careers are stalled because they simply <u>do not</u> understand others."

- *Across the Board Magazine* (for Business Leaders)

INTRODUCTION TO PART ONE

Understanding Your Multigenerational Workforce

Part One of this book gives you a brief overview of the different generations that currently make-up a majority of the workforce. I conduct tons of seminars to help companies improve generation relations at work, so I can tell you with authority that understanding *what makes other generations tick* is critical for you, as a leader, to know.

If you plan to effectively lead a multigenerational team, you need to know what Boomers, Generation Jones, and Gen X are about. Generational differences can, and do, affect communication, problem solving, relationship building, retention, loyalty, and team morale. And, if the team you lead suffers from a high turnover rate or low productivity rate, your company's top brass are going to look at you as the problem.

Well-known corporations wouldn't hire me to do presentations about generations at work if it wasn't an issue for them. And, one other point: A lot of the Millennial clients who hire me as their Leadership & Career Coach struggle with navigating generational dynamics within their team, and/or with *their own* managers/supervisors.

The purpose of this section is to give you a brief snapshot about the employees and supervisors you will face, and maybe already are facing, so that you can (hopefully) understand why they are the way they are. These insights will also give you great tools for better engaging with each member of your multigenerational team...great leaders take the time to understand people!

And we know all the older generations are talking about *your* generation (in general terms) a lot at work these days...so let's take a moment to talk about *them*.

Please Note: The following information is based on broad generational similarities. Obviously not everyone is the same or shares the exact personal history and traits I'll be describing. But I can tell you that a vast majority of people who attend my presentations all totally relate to the descriptions I share about *their* generation(s).

C H A P T E R   O N E

GEN X: A Complex Generation (That There Aren't Enough Of)

Here's a reality to chew on: *Many of the conflicts that occur in the workforce today tend to happen between Millennials and Generation X.* Part of the reason for this is that you (Millennials) are close in age to them. This tends to create more of a *sibling* dynamic, versus a *parental* dynamic (like Millennials often have with Boomers). And, you are close enough in age so that you're often *competing* at work (for promotions, projects, recognition, etc.). But there are other reasons this (sometimes) challenging dynamic occurs, so let's discuss Gen X for a minute. You're bound to learn some insights that will help you as the leader of a team that includes Gen X employees.

Gen X Birth Years (approx.): 1966 to 1979, ages 30 to 43

Gen X History & Overview:

Gen Xers were raised in the heart of the 1970's – a time in our society where divorce rates skyrocketed. And mothers, even those still married, embarked on careers and (many) stopped being "stay at home moms". This is the era when the term "latchkey kids" was created, and the kids behind the latches were the Xers. For those of you not familiar with the term, it refers to coming home from school at a young age, and because no parent(s) were home from work yet, they were instructed to lock the doors while they were home without an adult.

This shift in history created a generation of young people who sought *family ties* with friends, and were forced to be independent and in a survival mode at an early age. And also during that time, our country was in the wake of the controversial Vietnam War and a severe economic bust. This had many of their parents raising Gen X kids with messages of "Be careful out there!" and "Don't trust authority!" and "Look out for yourselves!"

The result? Gen X tends to be a pretty cynical generation. And, being on the cusp of Gen X and Gen Jones myself, I can tell you that I can relate. Also, when I discuss this in seminars, most of the Gen Xers nod along in agreement. So I'm not just making this up.

Gen Xers don't have the easiest time with "team work", and often scoff at having to attend management and leadership training seminars. As a whole, *they like to be left alone to do what they do, and how they like to do it.* They often possess a cocked eyebrow at authority, which can make it really challenging for their bosses – especially if the boss is younger than they are (ahem, Millennial leader? Are you getting this?).

One other thing you possibly didn't know: Gen X introduced the term *work-life balance* into the workforce. Tired of watching the Boomers work endless hours, and even more tired of feeling like they needed to keep pace with them; their generation began to demand that employers respect an employee's life outside of work more. This whole concept seems to be getting more attention now that your generation has entered the workforce – but know it was Gen X who started the movement for everyone!

What You Need to Know As Their Leader:

Many Xers possess a curt communication style. I advise that you don't take this personally (unless they are downright rude), but rather *just be aware of it*. A majority of Millennials like to communicate a lot with their supervisors, and bring that desire with them into leadership roles (wanting to communicate a lot with their employees). But don't expect that to be embraced by all of your Gen X talent.

As a whole, Gen X isn't big on chitchat, and they're not overly into being warm and fuzzy with co-workers or bosses. They prefer a direct communication style/dynamic, and when annoyed, their non-verbal cues can be pretty obvious (meaning, they typically don't hold back on rolling their eyes, sitting back and folding their arms, or saying something with an obvious "tone" in their verbal delivery).

One other point: Their generation isn't real big on schmoozing or "doing lunch" at work. They tend to save that for their social life outside of work. Remember, they started the work-life balance trend. That was fueled by a strong desire to keep those two worlds separate. This is often the total opposite of what your generation wants…you seek the "work-life balance" but also like work to be a social place where you build close relationships and have fun.

Coach Lisa's Comments:

Again, Gen X personality traits are not things to take personally – simply being aware of them can make your life easier as their boss or co-worker. I suggest that you adjust your leadership style to work with their preferences. A good leader is *adaptive*, and is mindful of what makes each employee tick.

C H A P T E R   T W O

Generation Jones: Newly Defined, Massive & Influential

The term Generation Jones was coined and defined by a colleague of mine, Mr. Jonathan Pontell, a leading social commentator. According to the research he (and others) has shared, this demographic is defined by people born between 1954-1965; thus currently comprising the largest adult population in the US (26% = 53 million people). And, prior to his research, they had always been lumped together with the Boomer generation. But their upbringing and history was significantly different from the (older) Boomers (born between 1942-1953).

Generation Jones Birth Years (approx.): 1954 to 1965, ages 44 to 55

Gen Jones History & Overview: While many Boomers were protesting Vietnam, attending Woodstock, and kicking off the sexual revolution, Gen Jones was attending elementary school, and hanging out at home watching *The Brady Bunch*, playing Pong, and cooking with Easy Bake Ovens.

As a member of Gen Jones myself, I can say I was relieved when I came across Jonathan's research. I had never fully identified with either Gen X or the Boomers. But, depending on what generational birth range you looked at, I was either considered a really old Gen Xer or a really young Boomer. His research identifying Generation Jones expressed things I could totally relate to. My first reaction was, "Finally! I have a generational identity that really does describe *me*!"

Many Gen Jonesers were still too young to make an impact as leaders back in the turbulent 70's and booming 80's, so they were forced to wait for their turn in the spotlight. And, now, that time has come. Born in 1961, President Obama is a Joneser and many senior executives in the workforce now are. His leadership style, and the personality traits we all witness in media interviews, is very similar to the Gen Jonesers who are my colleagues. A vast majority of them seem to be: Calm yet yearning, direct yet respectful, personable yet professional, extremely approachable yet slightly distant, and very outwardly confident yet internally obsessed in self-evaluation.

Many younger Jonesers were raised with a Mom at home and a Father working. And their early childhoods were filled with a sense of innocence. During the time my Boomer cousins were in their teens protesting war and/or getting caught up in Beatle mania, I was into watching cartoons, riding my bike, skateboarding, and playing with Barbies.

What You Need to Know As Their Leader:

In general, Gen Jonesers share a quiet optimism, confidence and patience. You'll find that they possess strong characteristics of both Gen X and Boomers: One day they'll want to "do lunch" with you, but the next they'll only want short, succinct communication with you. Sometimes they'll be focused on wanting to work as a team and then switch to wanting to work solo on a project. And from a work ethic standpoint, members of Gen Jones often follow the path of the Boomers – *they tend to be workaholics.*

Coach Lisa's Comments:

I realize the overview I provided of Generation Jones may actually make them seem schizophrenic! But don't let that scare you when having to manage them (or be managed by one). They tend to be fair, personable, diplomatic, and willing to go the extra mile. And their "traditional" Boomer-type values also foster loyalty in them as employees.

Focus on respecting their long-time professional experience, seek their input, value their knowledge, and maintain an open dialogue with them about *how your leadership style* works with their personal preference(s). You'll see they will respect you as a young leader if you avoid thinking you know everything...and if you avoid disrespecting their value to the team just because they are 20-30 years older than you.

Please Note: For more detailed information about Generation Jones, I encourage you to visit Jonathan Pontell's website(s): JonathanPontell.com and GenerationJones.com. You'll be working with this generation for 10-25 years, so you better get to know them!

C H A P T E R   T H R E E

Boomers: The Seasoned Generation at Work

The mass Boomer retirement (aka: Boomer Brain Drain) is something that will impact the workforce for decades. The amount of knowledge and experience going with them is something companies are scrambling to harness. Yes, companies are also focused on recruiting and retaining Millennials to build their future workforce, but almost as much time is being spent on how to retain Boomers longer. Why? Not only do the companies need the headcount, but they also need them to share their knowledge with as many younger employees as possible.

Sure, many of you know how to bring new technology into the workforce at lightning speed (and many Boomers have no desire to text or fully understand social media). But much of what they can teach you in terms of navigating the political waters of the workforce, making wise career decisions, building relationships, learning the ropes on how to do your job at hand (marketing, engineering, accounting, HR, etc.), are invaluable. And if you are not currently seeking a Boomer at work to be (one of) your mentor(s), you're doing yourself a disservice as a professional and as a young leader.

Boomer Birth Years (approx.): 1942 to 1953, ages 56 to 67

Boomer History & Overview:

The Boomers began to arrive during a time when things in the U.S. were going really well. We were at the tail end of WWII, the economy was booming, and most Boomers spent their adolescence in the innocent 1950's. The term "nuclear family" was created during their generation, and referred to having a traditional family up bringing (a Mom at home and a Dad working).

During their growth years, Boomers saw their parents stay at one job for a very long time, witnessed those companies take good care of their parent(s) in retirement, and saw the work ethic of their parents and grandparents. This was an era where you worked hard, didn't complain, tolerated a job even if you didn't love it, and felt loyalty towards the company that employed you.

As the Boomers began to enter the workforce, they brought these traditional values with them. There are many people over 50 years old who have been at the same company for 25+ years. So this changing workforce dynamic of "moving around a lot", and companies not being loyal to their employees, is pretty startling to many of them.

What You Need to Know As Their Leader:

Many Boomers "grew up" in the workforce at a time when you didn't question authority. You did your job and kept your mouth shut. Because of this, younger generations have a hard time adjusting to the Boomer trait of "putting process ahead of results". This means that even though you may have a more efficient way of doing something, a Boomer may be more concerned with keeping the process as-is because "that's the way the company has done it for years".

But on a positive note, Boomers also tend to be much like Millennials in terms of being personable and optimistic. They also enjoy relationship building, and appreciate business invitations to have lunch or dinner. Remember, they were doing martini lunches when it wasn't frowned upon (and you were a kid), so don't hesitate to offer invitations to them for socializing outside of the office.

And, again, their values tend to make them very loyal and willing to go the extra mile at work. So, if you do manage people between 56-67 years old, they could be the most loyal and hard working team members you'll have.

Coach Lisa's Comments:

Don't disregard a Boomers input just because you think they're "out of touch" with the latest technologies. They bring much more to the table than technical expertise (or lack thereof). You can learn, *and will learn*, from team members who have 25+ more years of work experience than you.

As a leader with Boomer employees, I recommend you consider setting up a *reverse mentor program*. I've suggested this to many clients and it works really well. This means you team-up younger employees with Boomers, and they can assist the Boomers with: Learning new software systems your company installs, understanding different social media strategies, reviewing new tech tools for communication, etc.

You can also arrange casual lunch & learn workshops where Millennials or Gen Xers do training on new technology and *any* employees can attend. There are many people younger than Boomers who also struggle with technology and learning new processes, so make a comfortable, non-judgmental, environment for everyone.

These suggestions are ways that you, as a young leader, can make your Boomer employees more comfortable, and keep them productive and enthusiastic. It's a proven fact that we ALL begin to lose our ability to quickly and easily learn/understand complex processes or tools past the age of 45. And it becomes more of a challenge as we push 60. So be aware of this and support your Boomer team members. *And be sure to tap into everything they can teach you!*

C H A P T E R   F O U R

20 WAYS MILLENNIALS WILL CHANGE THE WORKFORCE

Courtesy of Ryan Healy

Ryan Healy, himself a Millennial, is the Co-Founder of BrazenCareerist.com, a career management tool for next-generation professionals. Recently, Ryan was named one of the country's top Human Resource thought leaders by World at Work and Accenture. He is a recognized workplace expert for the young workforce, and has appeared as a spokesperson for Millennials on (partial list): *60 Minutes, 20/20* and *National Public Radio.* Formerly, Ryan was a Financial Consultant for IBM Global Business Services.

Authors Note: *The following list was written by Ryan and has not been edited. He wrote numbers 1-10 before the financial crisis hit in the fall of 2008, and then went on to write another list of ten insights (numbered 11-20 in this chapter) AFTER the economic crisis was in full tilt, and after the election of President Obama.*

He published both lists on his blog and received tons of comments from people of all generations – some supporting his insights and some not. I found his ideas and observations to be extremely interesting and felt they'd be appropriate to share in this book. As a young leader in the workforce, you may enjoy his perspectives on how your generation will impact the workforce...and remember, Ryan is a Millennial, too!

1. We'll Hold Only Productive Meetings: Meetings are important, sometimes. A good meeting will pull everyone to the same page while motivating them to get the work done. It's rare when that should take more than 30 minutes. Efficiency is the name of the game with Gen Y. We know that a drawn out meeting really means, "We have no idea what we're doing," and these time suckers actually halt productivity and stifle creativity, the qualities that they were supposed to encourage. As soon as Gen Y is running the show, watch wasted meeting time drop dramatically.

2. We'll Shorten the Work Day: The workday is eight hours. Or so they say. A real workday for most of us, if you include the commute, lunch, breaks and maybe dinner, is at least 10 hours. But how many hours of the day are actually spent doing real work? I would guess about half. To truly balance work and life, you cannot mess around and waste time at the office. Gen Y knows this. We're productivity machines; we will figure out how to get as much done in six to seven hours as the average boomer does with his eight.

3. We'll Bring Back the Administrative Assistants: Back in the day, nearly everyone had a secretary. These days, you have to be a CEO or high-level executive for a Fortune 500 company to have an assistant. Sure, this saves the company a ton, but Generation Y won't stand for it much longer. We recognize the value of time. Two extra hours per day not filing papers and mailing checks adds up to over 500 extra hours per year that we can spend with family and friends. Even if it comes out of our own pocket, Gen Y will cough up the extra dough to get a part time or virtual assistant.

4. We'll Redefine Retirement: Retirement is dead. It's dead for a number of reasons, including the issues with social security and middle class America's inability to save any money. But Gen Y will figure out how to save money to retire–we're already demanding 401K's and excellent benefits. However, we will re-invent retirement by taking multiple mini retirements instead of calling it quits a few years before its time to croak. Maybe in our late twenties we'll take a few months just to travel the world. Then, as we approach parenthood and our kids grow up, we'll take a year off to enjoy time with our family. Then we'll return to work, refreshed and ready to go. When we hit 65, it will be the new 45 and we'll have a solid 15 to 20 years left before we take our final, very brief, mini retirement.

5. We'll Find Real Mentors: Gen Y is obsessed with career development. We understand the importance of great mentors and we seek them out. The problem is that many older workers weren't effectively mentored and they don't always know how to mentor Gen Y. When it's Gen Y's turn to be senior mentors, we'll know how. As we seek mentors now we'll learn what works and what doesn't. And from the time we enter the workforce until the time we're senior employees, the smartest Gen Yers will figure out how to mentor up. We will teach our older co-workers about new technologies and the power of online communities, and they will respond kindly by guiding us through the insane office politics that exist everywhere.

6. We'll Restore Respect to the HR Department: Ten years ago, human resources got no respect. Today, companies are just beginning to see the importance. Gen Y recognizes that people make the company successful. Maybe it's not tangible and maybe it's not easy to see the direct ROI on keeping people happy, but happy people create successful organizations. All you need to do is take a look at Google, the company that's quickly taking over the world, to see that happy people are successful people and successful people make a lot of money for themselves, and for the company. HR is not a cost center, its vital to the bottom line.

7. We'll Promote Based on Emotional Intelligence: For some reason, companies assume that when you pay your dues and you know the business, you can be a manager. They're wrong. The truth is that seniority does not make a good manager. People skills make a good manager. By the time Gen Y is running the world, we will be smart enough to promote people to managers because they can manage, not because they've worked for ten years. For managers, personal work must come a distant second to developing employees both personally and professionally. If you can't help others, you don't deserve a promotion to manager and you will be left behind.

8. We'll Continue to Value What Our Parents Have to Offer: Sure, Gen Xers can laugh about it now, but Gen Yers respect our parents, and our parents are interested in every part of our lives, even when we're 30. Don't be surprised to see Gen Y employees giving their parents a tour of the office and calling up mom and dad for a little advice on their lunch break. It's not about being babied or refusing to grow up, it's about a level of mutual respect that Gen Y has for our parents and our parents have for us. My mother is coming to visit in a couple weeks, and guess what our plan for the day is? A tour of the office and a couple hours of work for each of us before we go out and do the tourist thing.

9. We'll Enjoy Higher Starting Salaries: Sure, Gen Y is interested in volunteering; putting a halt to global warming and all that other good stuff, but we're not our idealist parents. We watched our parents get laid off and we know that companies look out for themselves, so we do the same. Gen Yers will gladly accept a higher starting salary than promises of raises and promotions that we may never see. Additionally, all we have to do is go to Payscale.com or some other site to find out what the average starting salary is. Then we will ask for more, and we'll probably get it, because we know we can get it elsewhere if your company won't give it to us.

10. We'll Re-invent the Performance Review: Semi-annual or annual performance reviews do not work. Gen Y wants constant feedback. If we're only at a company for two years, we cannot wait for our one-year review to find out how we're doing. Gen Y will invent the on-the-spot performance review. The smartest companies will train their managers in giving frequent feedback, and the companies that don't will get a quick reality check when their Gen Y employees demand them. Spot reviews lead to consistent improvement, and consistent improvement is what truly matters to Generation Y.

11. We'll Reduce Executive Compensation for Under-performing Companies: It's already happening. Obama put a $500,000 cap on executive pay at the banks that were bailed out. In 2007, the average CEO salary at the largest companies was more than $11 Million. It's hard to justify paying anyone that much. In some cases, these executives probably do provide more $11 million in value to their respective companies. And when that happens, they should be compensated for it. But having a CEO expect $11 million regardless of performance is just bad business. The Obama administration is setting the precedent, and as Gen Y takes power we will follow through and reduce executive compensation for underperforming companies.

12. Discussing Salaries Will Be Completely Normal: Transparency is king. You hear it everywhere these days. Social media is forcing companies to open up their doors and show the world what's really going on. Obama has promised budget transparency to the American public. And the vast majority of the world's under-30 population is living their entire lives online. Transparency is no longer an option. Websites like Glassdoor and Payscale let you compare your salary with others in the industry. My company, Brazen Careerist practices complete transparency. Even financial gurus like Suzie Orman say it's great for business. As Gen Y continues to work our way up the ladder, it will just be a matter of time before companies of all sizes have transparent salaries.

13. Employees Will Be More Loyal Than Ever Before: Transparency does not just mean that everyone knows what everyone else in a company makes. It means that the company must educate their employees on everything that is going on. When Pepsi was ready to release their new "Gen Y Friendly" logo to the world, they wanted to make sure that their employees weren't surprised when they found it in the grocery store. So they invited their staff to a party and introduced the product. The employees were excited and they felt like the company actually cared about them. When employees feel like they matter and the company thinks about them first, they feel a sense of pride and true loyalty to a company. Expect to see this trend continue as Gen Y comes of age.

14. There Will Be Less Mass Layoffs, But More Pay Cuts: When someone feels a true sense of pride and loyalty to their company, they're more likely to figure out a way for everyone to pull through when times are tough. We watched our parents and our friend's parents being laid off when we were young and we're going through it now. We know the hardship that comes with it. Don't be surprised to see across-the-board pay-cuts instead of mass layoffs when times get tough. Start ups do it all the time – my company did it without thinking twice. And it's already happening at large corporations; HP just instituted a 5% or more across-the-board pay-cut rather than lying off hundreds. When you're part of a team, you want that team to succeed, and you'll do what's necessary to survive. And as we all know, Generation Y is the ultimate team player generation.

15. We'll Truly Get Over the "Punch Clock" Mentality: It's easy to say you have a progressive workplace and that you don't care what hours people are actually working at the office or what they do outside of work. But the truth is, companies care and people care. At the typical company, everyone notices what time someone leaves the office and what time people get in. We're still stuck in a workplace that was designed around producing widgets on an assembly line. As life moves more and more online, and new tech-nologies are invented that allow traditional offices to be truly optional, the punch clock mentality will slowly disappear. By the time Gen Y is ready to retire, people won't even know what a punch clock is, and maybe then we will finally be working in the environment that knowledge workers are meant to work in.

16. Independent Contractors Will Become Part of the Team: Nearly every company hires independent contractors to work for them. Contractors are great. They don't require health insurance and you don't have to pay the extra taxes. But they're often treated very differently than traditional employees. As more people develop skills that allow them to be effective independent contrac-tors, and some form of universal healthcare is finally adopted, companies will begin to think of their contractors as their employees. When Brazen had a big budget, we worked with a ton of contractors. When people asked how many employees we had, I would always mention that our team felt much larger because of all the freelancers. As the number of independent contractors increases, they will become a vital part of the team.

17. Corporate Branding Will Work in Conjunction with Personal Branding: Companies spend a lot of money on branding. They throw huge budgets at PR firms and super bowl ads. It usually results in a ton of brand recognition. But brand recognition is no longer enough. Consumers want transparency, conversation and experience. Generation Y doesn't want a company to talk AT us, we want to talk WITH a company. The only way for a company to talk with a person is to give employees the freedom to interact. It's already happening as people like Sharpie Susan are branding themselves as social media players and helping their companies in the process. Who knows exactly how this will play out, but as Gen Y invents new technologies and new marketing strategies, corporate branding will never look the same.

18. Leadership Will Be a Team Effort: Jack Welch was a larger than life CEO. Everyone knew who he was and his personal brand may have been just as big as GE's brand. In *Good to Great*, Jim Collins determined that dominant CEOs like Jack Welch actually have a lower than average ROI during their tenure. This is because CEOs need to be respected and admired by their employees, and they need to be selfless and always thinking about the organization. As a team-oriented group, Generation Y will not stand by and watch one person insert his will on the company. We will figure out a new form of leadership, where one person is the decision maker, but leading is a team effort. With all the new social technologies, there will always be a place for people with huge personal brands and huge personal egos. They will make a lot of money and still be well-known, but they won't be the ones running large organizations.

19. We Will Really Know People Before We Hire Them: I can't tell you exactly how they will look, but sooner than later, resumes will be extremely different. It's not because a hard copy piece of paper is outdated, it's because people are becoming more and more complex. Resumes were created when people went to school, graduated, got a job and maybe another job. But today people blog, job-hop and have multiple hobbies outside of work. We live our lives online. It's too limiting to judge someone based on one sheet of paper. Social technologies give employers a window into people's souls. As Gen Y become responsible for hiring decisions, you can bet we will know almost everything we possibly can about someone before we give them an offer.

20. Entry-Level Employees Will Be Students and Teachers: In the old days, entry-level employees had to pay dues before they moved up. This makes sense – it's impossible to know how a job or an industry works when you've never been there before. Young people had everything to learn and nothing to teach. Things are different now. For the first time in history, the youngest people in the workplace have the most knowledge about a very important topic – technology. And get this; we want to teach our bosses and managers how to use these technologies. This trend will continue. Young people will stay on top of the newest useful technologies. As Gen Y grows up, cross-mentor programs will be instituted. Old will teach young and young will teach old. Sounds like a great environment to me.

PART TWO

How to Become a Respected & Influential Millennial Leader at Work

"Outstanding leaders go out of the way to boost the self-esteem of their personnel. If people believe in themselves, it's amazing what they can accomplish."

— Sam Walton
Founder of Wal-Mart (opened his first store in 1962)

INTRODUCTION TO PART TWO

How to Become a Respected & Influential Millennial Leader at Work

Part Two of this book is comprised of (8) chapters that are intended to provide you with principles, tips and strategies on how to be an effective and influential young leader in the workforce. And let me just say, there are many people, much older than you, who still don't have a grip on their leadership style (and don't even think about it), and struggle because of it. It truly amazes me how many people don't take the time to improve their leadership skills, and then wonder why they have on-going employee issues, suffer from turn over in their department, and never feel as though people respect them at work. And what's the root cause of this? Themselves! They don't take responsibility for their actions, and continue to think everyone else has a problem.

I don't want that to be *you*. The earlier you can start to learn about leadership, and begin to hone your personal style, the better off you'll be. And, the better off everyone around you will be. I don't care whether you are currently working in the mailroom or as a receptionist, or in a high profile management role, or still in school; developing your leadership mindset needs to start now!

So if you're aspiring to be more than just a cog-in-the-wheel at work, or in the world, keep reading. People with leadership skills and a leadership mindset, stand out and make a difference.

I will warn you that some of what you'll read in this section may seem a bit like "psycho-babble", but it is all about *the mind*; your mind! And as you read this section, take time for self reflection. Ask yourself things like: Do I currently do that? Do I handle situations like that? Can I improve my way of doing this? Will that tip or principle benefit me? How can I apply this info?

This really is all about you. So don't just *read* the information; *internalize* the information and learn from it! And, remember, none of this will help you, in any way, if you don't *take action* on it. That's like reading a weight loss book but then never actually trying the diet and fitness plan outlined in it.

Okay, I'll get off my soap box…let's jump into Part Two: *How to Become a Respected & Influential Millennial Leader at Work.*

CHAPTER FIVE

The Definition of a Leader & 6 Steps to Thinking Like One

What is a leader? Are they born or made? Is a leader someone with the right genetics for the role or are the skills to motivate, inspire, and engage something that can be learned?

The term "a natural leader" is applied to many successful business people...but what does it mean exactly?

Sure, some natural leaders are born that way. A quick visit to a nearby sandbox can provide an eye-opening education. Even at the tender age of three or four, instinctive leadership abilities are demonstrated as one child wrangles the others into group play, divides the assets (like shovels), and keeps the play area humming along nicely building an integrated series of sand piles, roads, etc.

There is certainly dramatic evidence about innate leadership abilities, it's true. But there is equally dramatic evidence, however, that the skill-set required to lead is one that *can be learned and mastered by anyone*...even someone who has never shown any signs of leadership traits.

Fake It Until You Make It...But That Gets You Only So Far!

Many see a leader as the person who *takes charge*. This leads to the discovery of a psychology tool used by leaders in business, politics, and every imaginable arena of human pursuit: the power of perception. If you want to be perceived as a leader, act like a leader. Leaders speak authoritatively, even when they may feel tentative. Leaders offer ideas, even when they're not certain others will approve.

But does the person who takes charge always deserve the power? Nope. Unfortunately, people who possess the outward attributes of leadership – a powerful presence, a strong verbal style, etc. – may not really have what it takes on the inside. So while it is important to act like a leader so that people will perceive you as such, it's equally important that you don't fake your way up the ladder with a hollow leadership façade that you won't be able to maintain. Trust me, it won't take long for those around you to know you're faking it...and that's when the backlash begins.

That is why it's so important to get past posing as a leader, and start truly being one. Using a loud voice, bossing people around, forcing your ideas on people, not listening to others, only (really) caring about yourself, and being caught up in your title/position, are all *respect killers*. They may get you into a leadership role, but they won't keep you in one.

Quite honestly, if this sounds like you, it's time for an attitude adjustment. As you continue to read this chapter and book, you'll quickly see that effective and respected leaders are totally the opposite of what I just described.

Defining Terms

In order to become a leader, it's important to first define the goal. So, *what is a leader?* The answer is complex and, more importantly, evolutionary. The skills and attributes that defined a business leader during the Industrial Revolution are certainly different than those defining a captain of industry in the Computer Age. Or are they?

In truth, the single most important defining characteristic of leadership is actually quite constant: A leader is someone whose knowledge (competence), moral compass (character), and personal performance values (ethics), <u>inspire trust in others</u>. To achieve that end, you must first trust (and respect) yourself. But I'm not talking about having a big ego; most people with big egos are really insecure and not driven by a very strong moral compass, and often don't care about others. And, more importantly, they may be the leader but they're not necessarily a *respected* leader.

6 Steps to Thinking like a Leader

We've all heard the phrase "You are what you eat", but it is really more accurate to say, "You are what you think." How you receive, process, and respond in your head to what's going on around you will determine how you act in reality. But more than anything, thoughts influence how you act, react, look, and sound in any given situation, especially in a leadership role.

Self-image comes from within...from your thoughts. So does self-confidence. These two key leadership attributes are things we create for ourselves by learning to control our thoughts. You may have heard the term *Reactive Mind*, coined by L. Ron Hubbard, the founder of Dianetics. Hubbard claimed that the *Reactive Mind stores impressions of past events, which occurred while the person was unconscious or otherwise not completely aware.*

I'm not a Hubbard groupie, but I do like this little nugget from his philosophy. It's the idea that we frequently *react without thinking, and often inappropriately.* Rather than respond to the current "real" situation we're in, our reactive minds make a *habitual response.* This knee-jerk reaction is influenced more by something that happened in the past rather than what is happening in the present.

At first glance, it would seem that choosing a response based on experience makes sense. It's the essence of learning. A child who is accidentally burned learns to stay away from fire. That's good. The problem arises when that child continues to avoid fire in even a controlled and safe situation – say the candles on a birthday cake. *The response is not appropriate to the situation, even though if feels right.*

Thoughts that <u>factor in</u> past experience, without assessing the real-time facts are counter-productive. Unfortunately, these hot-wired thoughts are frequently centered on negative self-image and undermine self-confidence. It's unfortunate because how you see yourself will influence how others see you and respond to you.

Here's the bottom line: It is impossible to be an effective leader of others when you are stuck in the past mentally and feel haunted by failure. Leadership is all about image and how others perceive you; but not fake! It is the natural outgrowth of the positive self-image that you have created on the inside, not an artificial persona that you put on like a raincoat. If you want others to believe in your competence, you must exude a self-confidence that gives them a reason to do so.

With the right thoughts as your foundation, there's nothing you can't accomplish. The goal then is to <u>take action to control your mind</u> and turn it into a reliable support system. "But how?" you may be wondering.

The first step is to take an inventory of your thoughts and see what your mind is manufacturing each day. You think I'm kidding? Nope. I often require my coaching clients to do this, and it's very helpful. You can't start to control your mind, versus letting it control you, if you don't start to see patterns and really start to "know you". And if you think this seems like a waste of time, think again. Some of the most well known and respected leaders I know have done this, and continue to do this. It gives them clarity, keeps them grounded and in-tuned with themselves, and that enables them to lead effectively.

So, here's the deal, the same way that a dieter keeps a food journal to gain insights into their eating patterns; you should consider keeping a **Thought Journal**. In your "mental diary", which can be a handwritten paper journal, Word doc, or a private blog (that others can't access), focus on these questions daily:

- **What's going on inside your head?**
- **What things are on your mind throughout the day?**
- **Are your thoughts generally positive or negative?**

You may have a general impression of your mindset, but you'll never know what's *really* happening until you have written down your thoughts and examined them. You may be shocked at how often you're shooting yourself in the foot with a self-negating thought!

Now comes the interesting part. At the end of the day, look at each negative thought and work to reframe it into something positive. This isn't as hard as it may appear. For example:

- Negative Thought: I've wasted 3 days learning this software app!
- Re-framed: Every day I'm getting more proficient with new technology and tools!

This isn't "happy talk" or lying to yourself. It is merely putting a more positive, a more *hopeful,* spin on the situation. By recognizing that you are becoming *more* proficient, you are opening the door to the fact that you will one day achieve mastery.

Key point: Hope and optimism are vital to leaders. Hope and

optimism help keep them focused on possibilities which can prevent them from becoming mired in any immediate crisis. Your mind can be a breeding ground for toxic negativity, or it can be fertile soil where positive solutions grow.

Here is the *Six Steps to Thinking Like a Leader:*

Step 1 – Take Charge: Negative thoughts are powerful, but you can keep them from running amok inside your head and influencing your behavior. Make a commitment to control what you think about. This means making a *daily effort* to consciously program positive thoughts or affirmations into your mind.

Step 2 – Watch Your Language: Would you talk to other people the way you talk to yourself in your head? You wouldn't dare! Use the word "should" as infrequently as possible. Treat yourself with the same respect and dignity you'd treat anyone else in your life...but that doesn't mean you should give yourself a free ride.

For example, instead of thinking, "I'm bad about not holding staff meetings consistently," reframe the thought as "I will schedule staff meetings every Monday at 9:30 am, and that will start next week." That way you're *talking* action and that means you're more likely to *take* action.

Step 3 – Remember the Good Times: One of the most insidious thoughts that invade a leader's mind is "What if?" The more creative you are, the more terrifying these worst-case scenarios will be, as you imagine computer network failures, supply chain disasters, personnel flare-ups, and other situations that could overwhelm you. You can't see into your future, and that's scary.

But here's a suggestion: Why not <u>think about your past</u>

successes instead of past failures? Empower yourself with real memories of the past and all the things you've achieved. Make a list of all the obstacles you've hurdled in the past and the tough situations where you've come out on top. This will be your go-to mental "safe place". It's where you should turn your thoughts whenever you start to doubt your capabilities to remind yourself that you have successfully handled challenges and obstacles before.

As a young leader, or even as you become a veteran leader with more experience, you will always be faced with challenges that seem unbelievable. And, as with most people, you'll get scared and wonder how the heck you're going to handle the situation. This is where having the "safe place" comes in very handy. As a leader, you may often find yourself feeling alone and having to boost yourself up. It is critical to your success to be able to *empower yourself* during those challenging times.

Step 4 – Let Go: When a difficult situation arises, do you deal with things coolly on the outside, but spend the rest of the day raging on the inside? The fact that you were able to mask your emotions may seem positive, but it's not really. It's exhausting to be "angry on the inside". Harboring resentment is a huge drain that zaps your mental, emotional, and even your physical reserves. It's also pointless.

Unless you can take action to rectify a situation, there is no point in thinking about it. It doesn't matter who was right and who was wrong. What matters is what you can learn from it and how you can use what you've learned in the future. Beyond that, what's past is past.

Step 5 – Set a "Mental" Training Schedule: Unused thought patterns, like unused muscles, can get creaky and out of shape. The best way to avoid mental atrophy is with regularly scheduled "workouts" throughout the day. Block out time each day to focus on the process of *right thinking* and <u>define a specific action you can take</u>.

Let's say you have a habit of thinking, "There's too much work!" Make a deal with yourself that from 1PM until 3PM, if that thought comes into your mind, you'll immediately switch your mindset and think to yourself, "I, along with my team, am working hard to meet the deadline and we will make it." Before long, you'll create a habit and your mind will automatically make the switch-over to positive thoughts without any conscious help from you.

Step 6 – Acknowledge Progress: Perfection is a goal, not a destination, when it comes to managing your thoughts. The real measure of success in this area is ongoing progress. Remember to acknowledge where you've been so that you can appreciate how far you've come instead of worrying about how far you have to go. With your Thought Journal, it will be easy to monitor and mark the genuine progress you're making.

A good way to re-enforce any positive effort – in this case a positive thought – is with a **tangible reward**. If your Thought Journal reveals that you've gone 24 hours without a self-negating thought...or 3 days without holding on to anger...or haven't beaten yourself up with "shoulda-woulda-coulda" for a week...treat yourself to an extra latte or another music download. This way, you'll begin to unconsciously <u>associate your positive thoughts with positive experiences.</u>

Coach Lisa's Comments:

I told you this chapter may sound a bit like "psycho-babble", but it's important psycho-babble. I'm not just blowing smoke up your skirt (or pant leg). You can read a million books on leadership that provide general tips and principles on *how to lead others*. But if you don't really get to know yourself, and be honest with yourself about the self-sabotage dialogue that runs your mind, you'll struggle with **leading yourself**.

I want you to be a respected leader; not a feared leader (there's a difference). Feared leaders suffer a lot (unnecessarily). They don't trust or truly believe in themselves, they don't trust their team members, they live in a paranoid state, everyone is nice or respectful to their face but not behind their backs, their team members are rarely loyal, they have trouble attracting and retaining good employees, and they just tend to have a constant negativity "cloud" around them.

But truly respected leaders tend to experience the total opposite. Sure, they face major challenges, any leader does. But they don't get bogged down, and have all their energy zapped, with all the other crud I listed.

Keeping a Thought Journal is a great way to begin to see the thoughts that can negatively impact your journey as a young leader, so I hope you'll consider trying it! Even just for a week.

Another interesting exercise to keeping yourself in a positive frame of mind is the following (and it's another thing I encourage my coaching clients to do): Each night before you fall asleep, take a few minutes to write down, or mentally list, 4-5 things that acknowledge something positive about yourself. This can be "general" or something tangible (like a task you accomplished that day), that is about you. And each morning, while showering, driving to work, or whatever, list 4-5 things you have gratitude for. This list is meant to be about things "external": family, friends, co-workers, your neighbor, your dog, your house, your partner, etc. Focusing on acknowledging yourself, and focusing on gratitude, are great ways to start and end each day. And they are effective tools for keeping you grounded, thus elevating your (positive) leadership mindset.

C H A P T E R   S I X

23 Key Differences Between a Manager Mindset & Leadership Mindset

The confusion between the role of a manager and a leader has tripped up more than one business professional and cost many companies their very existence. Is 'the person in charge' automatically a leader? If you're managing other people, are you also leading them, by default? Just what is the difference between the two?

According to the current wisdom, managers are principally administrators; they write business plans, set budgets, monitor progress, and, yes, they manage people (but sometimes without the concept of an effective leadership mindset).

Leaders, on the other hand, <u>get organizations and people to change</u>. Most business executives and owners have a mix of management and leadership skills. And, quite often, both skill sets are necessary to run a successful business and team.

But typically, only the top executives can set direction in a company. Setting direction is different from setting goals. A goal is concrete and measurable: "We must sell 10 widgets by next

Tuesday." Direction is broader. Leaders set direction with a vision, a mission and operating principles that embody the company's direction and values.

Here is a key point that can settle confusion for you: Even if you just manage one person, regardless of what your role/title is, you are also a leader. Yes, you may be considered a "manager or supervisor" on paper, but you are leading, too. And even though your current position may not be one that "sets direction for the entire company", you are still a leader. And even if you currently don't manage even one person, you can take on leadership roles (heading up a project, like volunteering to plan the company's annual picnic). So whether you are actually in a true management role with employees, or assuming a short term leadership role for the annual picnic coordination, cultivating a leadership mindset is critical.

Whether someone is a Senior Vice President or an entry-level Sales Manager, they are both in management roles (managing other people). But successful managers are also successful leaders, and successful leaders stand out and move up!

So don't think "leadership" is something that only occurs once you're in an executive role. Your leadership mindset needs to start on Day One of your very first job.

Defining Terms

In general, **a manger** is a person that achieves company objectives through the actions and efforts of subordinates. A manager provides feedback to staff and serves as a liaison between executive and employees. A manager controls resources and expenditures, but his/her powers are defined by the organizational structure, which also defines the amount of influence managers have over subordinates.

A leader is the person that **sets company objectives and**

makes decisions that other people follow; someone that guides or inspires others. Leaders apply the same practices that good managers use. However, unlike managers who provide feedback, leaders solicit it. Leaders listen to what their subordinates say and take the time to explore underlying issues. They help employees solve their own problems by *providing an environment where people know they are accepted.*

Both a manager and a leader may know a business reasonably well, but the leader must know the business to a finer degree and from a different view point. Leaders must grasp the underlying market forces that determine the past and present trends in the business's niche, so that they can generate a vision and strategy to bring about its future development and growth.

A crucial sign of a good leader is **an honest attitude towards the facts** and objective truth. Conversely, a subjective leader obscures the facts for the sake of narrow self-interest, partisan interest or prejudice. *Many managers sometimes fall into the trap of subjective leadership.* They become more intent on sending good news to the executive office to ensure their own professional health and longevity than to honestly deliver the bad news that should be a catalyst for needed change.

Art Imitating Life...Or Life Imitating Art?

The iconic Dilbert comic strip reminds us that in an age where the young may know more than their elders, staffers view their managers as people who don't understand things and who make life difficult for them with demands that make little sense. The manager in the Dilbert strip is a leader only in the sense that members of the technical staff are **forced to follow his directions**...no matter how inane.

And if you have never read Dilbert, then just watch a few episodes of the (current) hit sitcom, *The Office.* Steve Carell's character, Michael Scott, is the manager (aka leader) of the regional office. And although his title is "Manager", and he's supposed to be their leader, he doesn't possess one good leadership quality in his body. Although funny on TV (I love that show), it's not funny if someone like that is your boss in reality.

Rotten managers have been the focus of jokes forever in TV, movies, comic strips, etc. And, even worse, they have been the focus of jokes in reality, too. Do you really want to be one of *those* managers? Reality check: If whenever you walk into a group of your employees and everyone stops talking, you probably are. If your employees don't have much to say to you, you probably are. If your team always seems to have low morale and enthusiasm, except the week before you go on vacation, you probably are. If your employees quit a lot, you probably are. And if any of this remotely describes what you're experiencing as a young leader, I'm glad you are reading this book.

Good leaders make people want to achieve their very best, rather than just meeting a day-to-day objective. Leaders with a knack for <u>setting realistic goals, providing guidance and feedback and empowering others</u>, gain **the respect and support** of their staff.

A *manager stuck in a management mindset* basically directs resources to complete predetermined goals or projects. For example, a manager may engage in hiring, training, and scheduling employees in order to accomplish work in the most efficient and cost effective manner possible. And a manager is considered a failure if he/she is not able to complete the project or goals with efficiency or when the cost becomes too high.

On the other hand, *a manager with a leadership mindset* within a company *develops individuals* in order to complete predetermined goals and projects. A leader develops relationships with his/her employees by building communication, evoking images of success, and by eliciting loyalty.

The Trust Factor

Perhaps most importantly, the trust a leader demonstrates in his/her staff builds the employees motivation and commitment. In fact, a leader that is honorable and trustworthy will always focus on *doing the right thing*, and their staff will willingly follow them anywhere! **Influence comes from trust**; from a person's expertise, integrity, and empathy as perceived by others. Maximum influence accrues to those who are strong in all three areas.

Management consists primarily of three things: analysis, problem solving, and planning. If you go to any management course it'll probably be composed of those three elements. But leadership consists of vision and values and the communication of those things. That ability to *create a vision* is another main difference between leadership and management.

The Good Book says, "Without a vision the people perish." And any good business bible will tell you that when a leader has no vision, companies perish, too!

It is tempting to see managers as drudges who feed the machine while leaders create visions of a better world. Some business experts criticize those who denigrate managers in order to elevate leaders, and praise managers for bringing order, stability, and predictability to the workplace. I totally agree with this. However, I just wish more managers would take on "leadership" traits when it comes to how they manage their employees.

I realize not every person in a company wants to be a senior executive or "lead" the whole business. But to not embrace some fundamental, effective leadership qualities within your management style, that will make your team happier and more productive, is BEING LAZY in my opinion.

Have you ever heard this saying: "People don't leave companies; they leave managers"? It has been around forever and there is a reason. I'm just sayin'.

23 Key Differences Between a Manager Mindset & Leadership Mindset:

The following list provides **23 Core Competencies** that define key differences between leaders and managers. And, as you'll see, leadership skills tend to be *flexible, responsive to change, and future-oriented.*

1. Leaders set a standard of excellence – Managers set a standard for performance

2. Leaders are policy-makers – Managers set standard operating procedures

3. Leaders seek employee commitment – Managers seek employee compliance

4. Leaders are proactive – Managers are reactive

5. Leaders create change – Managers maintain the status quo

6. Leaders take risk – Managers are risk-averse

7. Leaders are analytical decision-makers – Managers are intuitive decision-makers

8. Leaders value planning – Managers value action

9. Leaders are passionate – Managers are controlling

10. Leaders can lead people – Managers manage work

11. Leaders originate – Managers imitate

12. Leaders can create followers – Managers have subordinates

13. Leaders can think long-term – Managers think short-term

14. Leaders can set the direction – Managers plan the route

15. Leaders persuade – Managers supervise

16. Leaders develop strategies – Managers develop tactics

17. Leaders can make decisions – Managers implement policy

18. Leaders use personal charisma – Managers rely on bestowed authority

19. Leaders have a transformational style – Managers have a transactional style

20. Leaders make and break the rules – Managers implement the rules

21. Leaders are pathfinders – Mangers use old roads

22. Leaders give credit – Managers assign blame

23. Leaders care about what's right – Managers care about being right

Coach Lisa's Comments:

I'll keep this short. Managers that don't choose to embody important leadership qualities, suffer. And their employees suffer. And their companies suffer. Short sighted managers tend to focus on process and procedures, not people and vision. Leaders focus on the latter, first. Be a young manager who blends management skills with a leadership mindset, and you will succeed in any role, at any level, your career path takes you.

Now, let's talk about (7) Ironclad Attributes of an Exceptional Leader!

C H A P T E R   S E V E N

7 Ironclad Attributes of an Exceptional Leader

We all know much has been written on the subject of leadership and many business writers and motivational speakers have codified the attributes they believe are essential for leaders. Frequently, however, their descriptions focus upon traits that make a leader <u>personable, affable and well-liked.</u> It's nice to be liked, but: Leadership is not (just) a popularity contest. As a young leader, you will be faced with making decisions that won't make everyone happy. And that's okay. As long as your employees respect you, the ones who were not happy with your decision will (normally) get over it.

We live in a time plagued by cynicism and doubt, especially in regards to leaders and their motives, not only in corporate, but also government. This creates a special challenge for young leaders today who need to be trusted and respected in order to achieve the kind of 'popularity' that will enable them to achieve success, as well.

- **When the leader is respected**, which means they are at the very least trusted and probably liked as well, then this enables the leader to make proposals that followers will take seriously.

- **If the respect for the leader is strong**, then the followers will likely accept the solution being offered, even if they are not that convinced by the arguments that the leader is putting forward.

- **If the leader is <u>not</u> respected,** then people will follow them only if they see no other viable choice. But people will also (eventually) leave and seek a leader they do respect.

Someone Has to Follow the Leader

Almost everyone can describe the characteristics of an exceptional leader. Their descriptions may be based on a single great boss or on a collage of desirable features that they recognized in several leaders, but most people seem to have some idea of what's essential. But whatever else might be true about the role, you're not a good "leader" unless you have followers who respect you.

Leadership and management are often used in the same breath, largely because those who are appointed managers seek also to be leaders. I mentioned this in the previous chapter, but to recap (briefly), here are 2 key points:

- Managers have subordinates who obey commands in a basic transaction of <u>obedience in return for pay and conditions.</u> But when working for a manager without strong leadership qualities, who you don't respect, you (as an employee) are probably on the look out for another job. Basically, you just don't want to have to report to that person for very long.

- Good leaders, however, have <u>followers who choose to follow</u> them. And good leaders often have followers who are happy to be working for them, and compensation isn't their number one priority. They may even get job offers for more pay, but they just really like their boss and don't want to risk getting a new one that makes their lives miserable. And, yes, a bad boss makes your life miserable, so don't be one.

Role Reversal

The role of leader has many facets. Good leaders pay close attention to followers to ensure their ongoing motivation and if followers' buy-in decreases, then the leader must act to re-motivate them. This creates a leader-follower inversion, in which <u>the leader becomes the follower and vice versa.</u>

In this way, the roles of leader and follower are fluid. There is a constant shift of influence and motivation. A good leader, however, doesn't let the employees ultimately run the show. He/she always remains at the helm.

Pied Piper Power Play

A leader's *power* is not inherently good or bad, but just part of the equation. The **power dynamic** exists in leadership relationships because leadership is a process of influence, and <u>power provides influence potential</u>.

A leader's potential to influence others, to give them a reason to follow, flows from the leader's base of power. When used correctly, that power enables leaders to influence because the leader is *trusted, revered and/or considered an expert.*

An interesting comment on this comes from the arena...not the business arena, but the sports arena. Iconic NFL quarterback Joe Namath said, *"To be a leader, you have to make people want to follow you, and nobody wants to follow someone who doesn't know where he is going."*

What do successful leaders do to become effective Pied Pipers? What separates a leader from being a *basic* manager? And why do so many managers fail to live up to their leadership potential? The answer can be found, in part, in the attributes below.

7 Ironclad Attributes of an Exceptional Leader:

The following (7) attributes are reflections of character and personal integrity. They must be developed through self-discipline, time and pressure; they are not inherited and cannot not be "faked" successfully...at least not for long.

Attribute #1 – Sets High Standards: Leaders set high standards for their followers...and themselves. Successful leaders are consistent in demanding of themselves compliance with the standards that they espouse. Those who do not are only fooling themselves.

Attribute #2 – Lives Up to Those Standards: Leaders live up to the standards they have set. Nothing disqualifies a would-be leader faster than a **double standard**, one for them and another for those under their authority. Subordinates will quickly see through the duplicity, and loyalty will rapidly be replaced by *disgust, grudging obedience, and resignation letters.*

Attribute #3 – Mentors Those Who Follow: We all need guidance. However many mediocre leaders expect their followers to attain the standards set by their leadership without ever teaching them exactly how. Effective leaders, on the other hand, *invest themselves in their followers.* They make a concerted effort to communicate verbally not only <u>what is expected, but how to achieve it</u>.

Attribute #4 – Creates and Shares a Vision: Effective leaders are driven by a singular vision, not of what is, but of what will be. And they make sure that everyone around them understands and buys into that vision of *where the organization (and/or department) is going and what is necessary to attain that goal*. A splintered vision, or one that is implemented in a fragmented manner, will always result in **competing interests** within the organization, vying for resources, and each person thinking their particular function and sphere of effort is most important. This is when employee morale takes a plunge.

Attribute #5 – Makes the Hard Choices When Necessary: Effective leaders are characterized by a willingness to make the hard decisions when necessary...and sometimes under extreme pressure. Yet it is human nature that in the face of crisis, stall...keep all the options open. True leaders, however, don't stall. They assess and execute. They know that stalling, or going into a state of denial, just makes things worse.

Attribute #6 – Is Visible: In today's far flung organizations spanning continents, in your organization, whatever its size, do people really know where the buck stops? Do customers and staff alike have a clear and constant sense that someone, a real person, not voicemail, is really in charge? To command respect, which is a key component of trust and which is, in turn, the essential ingredient for creating followers, leaders must be highly visible. I know many mid-level managers who stay hidden in their offices...rarely meeting with employees, avoiding customers (thinking their sales reps can handle them), and basically avoiding anything that remotely looks like a "leadership" quality. Don't let that be you.

Attribute #7 – Instills Hope in Those Who Follow: The final attribute of successful leaders is their ability to instill hope. None of us can continue to grow, develop and perform at our highest potential without hope. Hope for success, hope for recognition and reward, and most importantly, hope that indeed we can make a difference in the long-term outcome. Hope supplies the essential fuel that enables the human spirit to continue moving forward, especially in the face of severe adversity. Be a young leader who instills hope in your team, as a group and as individuals. Even though this book is all *about you*, it's ultimately *for them*.

Coach Lisa's Comments:

Sure, the title on your business card, and your role within your company, will come with inherent respect. But it stops there. If you don't possess the attributes of a good leader, and work at becoming an effective one, on an on-going basis, the title on your card won't matter. Your co-workers, employees, and supervisors, will lose respect for you, and trust will disappear.

The only person that can maintain and build your status as an effective leader is you. And let me share something you may not be aware of: I talk to many older employees that are now managed by Millennials. And they are not resentful about it. But their frustration often comes from the fact that they (some, not all) say their young boss thinks they know everything, disregards other peoples' opinions, rarely asks for input from their teams, communicates in a condescending way, and tends to manage based on ego.

Now I realize there are many of *you* that have older bosses who manage the way I just described. But why should you be one of *them*? Why not work on your personal leadership style to only encompass traits that make you respected, well-liked, and effective?

The old school of traditional management and leadership styles has created a workforce where 60% of employees are dissatisfied and disengaged. I challenge you to bring in a new era of leadership that reduces that statistic! The attributes and principles in this book are best practices that the most effective leaders in our history, and those currently employed, possess.

This isn't rocket science; it's common sense! And the time to change the "negative" attitudes in the workforce is now, and that comes from good leadership…and you must lead the charge!

Suggestion: Are you clear on your personal strengths? Do you know how to utilize them effectively? Or do you spend more time focusing on how to fix your weaknesses?

Pick up a copy of this book, *Strengths Finder 2.0*. The updated edition came out in 2007, and it's a bestseller. It's really short, and each book also comes with a custom code for you to access an online assessment tool to determine your Top 5 strengths. And then you'll learn hundreds of strategies for applying them in your personal life and professional life.

Not only is this a great book, and exercise, that all young (aspiring) leaders should check out, but if you're already in a leadership role, get copies for each of your employees. All of you can read the book, take the online assessment, share your results, and have a group discussion(s) for team building. The more you and your team understand each other, the better!

C H A P T E R   E I G H T

14 Infallible Communication Strategies for Effective Leaders

As you know, within organizations there are many channels of communication that allow for an ongoing exchange of information: downward, upward, horizontal and informal.

Downward communications from supervisors to employees tends to flow in one direction, often discouraging response, whereas information sent **upward** from subordinates to superiors encourages feedback. Sharing information **horizontally** across department lines or among peers can help eliminate duplication and improve teamwork.

Meanwhile, the most informal communication channel, the social interaction among associates known as "the grapevine", can also be the most influential in business.

And at the center of all this information flow is the leader who understands that all *channels of communication are intrinsic to organizational performance*. But navigating the communication "waters" can be challenging for people of any age in a leadership role; which is why there are many managers/supervisors who don't tend to do a great job when it comes to communicating with their team members and co-workers.

In this chapter, we'll not only cover ways that you as a young leader can effectively communicate in "general" terms with your team (as a whole) regarding broad company decisions and initiatives, but also strategies to help you communicate with your employees one-on-one.

Mum's the Word

Decision-makers are often admonished to include people in the decision-making process because it enhances the likelihood of acceptance. But this is not always possible. As a leader, there will be times when you are involved in discussions with your superiors regarding issues that are often deep, nuanced and sometimes contentious. Simply put, the nature of the decision-making process and the features of the decision itself may make it impossible to keep your employees in the loop.

An example of this is when there is a manager's meeting where the CEO gathers you together to discuss the need to have company-wide lay offs. Or, the CEO wants to tell you the company may be acquired (or is planning to purchase another company). These can be discussions that the CEO does not want you to share with your team until further notice. And, certainly, you must respect this and not let info "slip" out to your employees. This is how rumors get started, and often times it's a loose lipped manager who gets the rumor mill moving. Don't be that person!

The real problem arises, however, after a confidential decision has been made. And you may find that as a leader, you will be responsible for sharing the news with your team about a new company policy (the top executives may not do it). Communicating a 'done deal' decision is difficult...and leaders, exhausted by the decision-making process, often give only minimal attention to doing it effectively.

The 'Hidden' Message

When we use the word *communicate*, we are referring not only to the words one uses to transfer factual information to others, but also to other unspoken "messages" that are sent and received. In a time of company or policy change, for example, an effective leader communicates the following "sub-texts" along with his/her message:

- A sense of confidence and control (or lack thereof) to employees.
- His/her own feelings about the change (within moderation and with tact).
- The degree to which he/she trusts the abilities of the employees to get through the change.
- A sense of purpose and commitment (or lack thereof).
- The degree to which he/she accepts the reactions and feelings of employees.
- Expectations regarding behavior that is seen as appropriate or inappropriate (i.e., rumor-mongering, back-room meetings, etc.).
- The degree to which he/she is connected to employees' situations and feelings, and/or is in-touch with them.

It is clear that if the leader communicates effectively, he/she will be sending messages that *decrease resistance, and encourage moving through the change* more effectively and positively. It is key, however, that although you can express empathy with your team members who express anger or confusion about the news; it is not okay for you to get on the "bashing bandwagon" along with them. Let them vent, but don't vent with them. Basically, answer any questions you've been ok'd to answer, but mainly focus on listening, being supportive, and providing encouragement.

Poor communication is repeatedly cited as a *key contributor in the failure of major change efforts*, so communication skills are increasingly regarded as a critical skill for leaders, particularly in situations where the leader is an instrumental driver of change.

Numerous studies also show that communication is closely tied to an organization's total effectiveness, which underscores why organizations need "communication champions" in order to be successful. And you, in a leadership role, will often be called upon to be one of those "champions"; for sharing great company news and not so great news with your team.

When It's Not All About the Company

Now let's get into solid tips for communicating "in general" with your team members, when it has nothing to do with telling them about some big companywide initiative. This is about how you communicate, day-to-day, with your employees.

Communication itself is not a goal; it's the means to an end. Great leaders consistently strive to strengthen their interpersonal communication competencies by **building and maintaining open, supportive, and collaborative relationships** with others in the organization.

In other words, communication is a two-way street with *effective* leaders participating in dialogues rather than *monologues*.

The essential point is that the professional world is now too complex for the leader to have all the answers. Effective leaders now realize that managing highly skilled talent in a way that gets the best out of people, and benefits the company, requires them to draw solutions out of people rather than restricting themselves to just selling their own ideas and solutions. To lead effectively, therefore, you need to be good at **active listening**. This means asking questions about what other people think and probing them on the pros and cons of their feedback. And, asking people for their opinions is the best way of showing that you value them; another essential leadership trait (if you want to engage and retain key talent).

In his book *Good to Great*, Jim Collins describes a successful leader as someone who excels at *knowing what questions to ask to draw good ideas out of their teams*. I strongly recommend you become good at that!

14 Infallible Communication Strategies for Effective Leaders:

1. Let Your Actions Speak As Loudly As Your Words: Make communications important to you personally. Take time to assess yourself on how well you communicate (up, down, around). Work on continuously improving your communication processes (written, oral, contextual, intuitive, and interpersonal).

2. Trust in Your Informal Channels: Employ an "open door" policy to gather information on what's actually happening (or not happening) in a quasi-social way. And remember that "shop talk" is an appropriate way to spend time communicating.

3. Don't Be Skimpy: When it comes to information, "too much is never enough." More communication is *always* better than less, especially during tough times when rumors may be flying around like a mosquito swarm. Plus, good communication is what *sells* changes and initiatives. And there's an additional benefit, too: Employees who feel well-informed tend to be more forgiving of the occasional error.

4. Ask When Telling Doesn't Work: When employees don't understand or aren't implementing a strategy effectively, don't *tell them louder*. Repeating the same information or guessing how to clarify what they need to know is fruitless. Instead, flip your communication approach from *talk to listen,* and ask employees to talk to *you.*

5. Talk Face to Face: In-person communications play a crucial role during times of uncertainty and change. As a leader, it's vital to display a willingness to address challenging questions, listen carefully, and respond quickly to sensitive topics.

6. Be A Fact-Finder: Make regular forays to find out what's being said, heard, and what's being forwarded electronically. Make a point to give people an opportunity to be listened to. When leaders engage with their followers, they're seen as a person who *understands what's happening, who is cognizant of feelings, and who doesn't have all the answers, but who is willing to listen, learn, and take action.*

7. Don't Go With the Flow...Facilitate It: Your job is to ensure the optimum flow of information in every direction. Communicate what you know, when you know it, as often as possible (when appropriate).

8. Tell the Truth: When bad news is candidly reported, an environment is created in which good news is more believable.

9. Don't Just Recite the Facts, Explain Them: In business, we worship at the altar of data...raw numbers and statistics that are easy to report, but not as easy to understand. This highlights a common reason for communication disconnect. Team members don't just want a recitation from their leader, they also want an interpretation from them: "What sense do you make out of this data (aka news)? What is your conclusion? Can you share your thoughts with us?"

10. Use Emotion: Storytelling is an important tool for leaders who want to connect on an emotional level with their employees. Personal stories illustrate to followers what the leader feels and why he/she feels that way. So not only can storytelling (using your own personal stories) communicate your point(s) better, but they can *humanize* you, and build bonds with your team.

11. Communicate with Groups: Effective leaders use group communications to ensure everybody hears the news at the same time, to encourage group discussion, to generate ideas, (perhaps) start the problem-solving process, and to increase the sense of team. In something like a lay-off situation, you can call a short group meeting to announce the lay-offs in general, then immediately meet individually with each staff member to inform them of their status (if it has been determined), OR to simply provide private discussions for each person to openly communicate with you about their fears, concerns, anger, etc.

12. Communicate with Individuals: One-on-one, private communication is valuable when the information being shared is likely to cause a high degree of emotions. Individual conversations also ensure that shyer people have a chance to express themselves to you. Having regular, one-on-one meetings with each of your team members is critical.

13. Communicate Verbally When Appropriate: Oral communication provides more opportunities for getting and keeping interest and attention, to use verbal emphasis, and the chance to listen to, and remove, resistance. And verbal communications are more likely to affect people's attitudes.

14. Communicate in Writing When Appropriate: Generally, the more emotional the issue, the more important it is to deliver the news verbally, preferably in-person. If it's information that is "light", like telling your team you want to take them to lunch next week, or that you'll be taking some vacation time next month, written is fine. But I know of a big company who sent out a "there will be cutbacks starting next month" mass email to all employees. Can you see what's wrong with written communication in *that* scenario?? The whole company freaked-out, had no idea about what types of "cutbacks", and all ran to their managers (this could be you) for an explanation...and they were already mad, scared, and in a panic. Suddenly you're dealing with "angry villagers", seeking answers, and you're in total damage control mode. So, your company may choose to drop news like that to the masses in writing, but whenever you have control of how information can be communicated, whether it's just to one employee, or to your whole group, be wise about how you do it.

Coach Lisa's Comments:

In my professional coach training, and in my coaching experience, I have found there are many principles of coaching that effective leaders can use, and do use, when communicating with employees. Basically, great leaders are also great coaches, even if they don't think of themselves as such.

That said, I'd like to share with you some solid communication tips pertaining to *Effective Listening & Effective Feedback* that will help you immensely:

Effective Listening:
- In the world of coaching, we're taught to listen 80% of the time and talk 20% of the time (I don't necessarily follow that ratio closely all the time, but you get the point). As a leader, that's a ratio you should also consider when meeting with an employee. You may have also heard that old saying, "You

were given 2 ears and 1 mouth…so use them accordingly". It really boils down to another great saying, "I never learned anything while I was talking".

- Did you know that we usually only can recall about 50% of what someone said immediately after they said it? That's because very few people are good at *active listening*, and are more focused on how what the person is saying impacts *them*, and formulating their response before the person is even done talking. <u>Focus on being an active listener!</u> Be totally attentive and tuned in to the person talking, and remain "present".

- Practice the use of *paraphrasing* once a person is done talking. This means responding with something like, "Just so I'm clear, what I heard you say was…" This keeps you on track, makes them feel heard and understood, and reduces the chances of miscommunication.

- Eliminate distractions! If you're communicating via phone, walk away or turn away from your computer so that you're not tempted to start checking email or work on a project. And if you're meeting with someone in your office, do NOT read email, text, IM or whatever while they are talking to you. That's rude, condescending, greatly reduces your chances of hearing them correctly, and can make the person feel totally disrespected and frustrated.

- Use the W.A.I.T. Principle: So often we interrupt people while they are talking. This happens all the time, and can be the foundation for ineffective communication and comprehension. So here's a tip to consider: Wait 10 seconds before responding to what someone just told you. This allows the person to have a few seconds to finish their thoughts and perhaps think of one more thing to add, and it gives you a few seconds to respond thoughtfully. Here is what the acronym W.A.I.T. stands for "**Why Am I Talking?**"

Effective Feedback: Providing good, effective feedback is often without judgment, and sometimes without your opinion (unless you are being asked your opinion).

- One tip is to ask the person *for permission* before giving the feedback. Sometimes your team member may simply want to be venting, and in a very emotional space, and you're on the verge of jumping into a whole dialogue filled with opinion and/or criticism. So by asking them "May I share some feedback with you?" gives them the opportunity to say "No, now wouldn't be good. I just wanted to vent". Or, if they say yes (and 99% of the time most anyone will), it can ground them to really hear your response because your "asking them permission" question gave them a moment to <u>prepare for listening</u>. This works really well. I do it all the time.
- Ask a lot of questions. Often what someone is expressing may not be the real issue or point, and you can help them by asking questions. Try to get past "how what they are saying makes you feel or impacts you", and focus on "them". As I mentioned before, getting good at questioning is a key trait of an effective leader.
- Try to listen to your employees without judgment. Just because you can't relate to what they are expressing, or don't agree, doesn't mean it's wrong. Hear everyone out (employees, co-workers, your boss, etc.), because you will learn more by doing that. By not always focusing on "you", and your ideas, comments and opinions, you will be known as an effective, and respectful, leader...and that's what we want!

C H A P T E R   N I N E

13 Leadership Tips for Problem Solving

Earlier in this section, leadership was defined as the ability to inspire, influence, and provide direction for people. But leadership is also a *system of approaches* to solving the problems of an organization in such a manner that the inspiration, influence, and direction come about in an effective and efficient manner.

As you read this chapter, please keep in mind that "problem solving" isn't just related to a company's challenges, but to your department's challenges, and to your own. And the challenges you will face, or are facing, can range anywhere from an employee who is not performing, to a process you have implemented that is not working, to goal's the company has established for your team that aren't being achieved. Regardless, being able to problem solve, for an issue of any magnitude, is key to being an effective leader.

Rational and Appreciative Inquiry Methods for Problem Solving

There are many approaches to problem solving, and choosing the right one depends on the nature of the problem, the people involved, and the dynamics creating the problem.

The more traditional method, a *rational approach*, is typically used, and involves steps such as:

- Clarifying a description of the problem
- Analyzing causes
- Identifying alternatives
- Assessing each alternative
- Choosing an alternative
- Implementing the alternative
- Evaluating whether the problem was solved or not

Another method, that requires more personal reflection, is *appreciative inquiry*. This approach asserts that problems and solutions are often the result of <u>our own perspectives.</u> Appreciative inquiry includes:

- Identifying our best times in a similar situation in the past
- Thinking about what worked best then
- Envisioning the outcome after the issue has been "fixed"
- Building from our strengths to work towards the vision of the solution

Many leaders use a combination of the two methods. Appreciative inquiry can act as a "personal empowerment" approach when you are feeling overwhelmed or insecure about a challenge you're faced with. Being able to tap into past experiences you've had where you were faced with a huge obstacle, which seemed too much to handle, but successfully pulled through, is key.

As a young leader, you will face challenges, large and small, that you will be expected to handle quickly and effectively. And, you'll need to rely on yourself to, not necessarily fix everything alone, but rather give yourself the courage to lead the charter to solving the problem.

This is hard for many leaders...they get fearful, can't muster up courage and personal strength, and therefore "avoid" issues...that often just get worse.

But once you've empowered yourself to "face" what is happening, you can use the *rational method* steps to start putting together your plan for taking action.

Problem Prevention

Small problems often precede catastrophes. In fact, most large-scale failures result from a series of small errors and failures, rather than a single root cause. These small problems often cascade to create huge ones. Accident investigators in fields such as commercial aviation, the military, and medicine have shown that a chain of events and errors typically leads to a particular major disaster.

Thus, *minor failures and small issues may signal big trouble ahead.* So it's very important that you don't stick your head in the sand, but actually pay attention to early warning signs.

Many large-scale business failures (whether companywide or in one small business unit) have long incubation periods, meaning that leaders have ample time to intervene when small problems arise, thereby avoiding a catastrophic outcome. Yet these small problems often go unnoticed, or someone sees them but doesn't want to "deal with it". That is why it is so important for you to not lead by fear! If your employees are scared to tell you things, because you always yell or threaten them, they won't. You'll create an environment where you don't know much about what's really happening, and you'll spend your career playing defense versus offense. And, trust me; being *proactive* tends to be a lot easier than being *reactive*.

View Problems as Opportunities

Most individuals and organizations do not view problems in a positive light. They perceive problems as abnormal conditions – as situations that one must avoid at all costs. After all, fewer problems mean a greater likelihood of achieving the organization's goals and objectives. As a result, many leaders do not enjoy discussing problems, and they certainly do not cherish the opportunity to disclose problems in their own department. They worry that others will view them as incompetent for allowing the problem to occur, or incapable of resolving the problem on their own.

Smart leaders, and/or organizations, perceive problems quite differently. They view small failures as quite ordinary and normal. They recognize that problems happen, even in very successful organizations, despite the best leadership talent and most sophisticated management techniques. These organizations actually **embrace problems**.

Good leaders view problems as opportunities to **learn and improve**. Thus, they **seek out problems**, rather than sweeping them under the rug. Don't be a sweeper!

13 Leadership Tips for Problem Solving:

1. Leaders First Envision Success: Leaders know that every problem has an answer; it just needs to be found. Worrying about the problem gets you nowhere, while working towards the answer will get you everywhere. Leaders control their attitude and focus on results.

2. Leaders Clarify the Problem: Leaders determine what's wrong by cutting through clutter and noise, and by focusing on the issues that are at the core of the problem.

3. Leaders Get the Facts: Leaders collect all the facts about the problem because they know that some problems are not as big as they seem. Fact-finding is an analytical, rather than an emotional task, so it is useful in other ways, too. When a follower comes to a leader with a problem, a good leader will start asking questions and gather the facts, *rather than engage in an emotional discussion*. Fact-finding is a process and you may have to dig deep to get to the real problem. Leaders are great at asking the right fact-finding questions. They're also adept at listening to the answers and "hearing" any sub-text that could illuminate the situation.

4. Leaders Decide Which Problems Need Solving: Leaders don't guess or assume when it comes to problem-solving. They decide where to focus their efforts based on the fact-finding step above. While every problem may have a solution, not every problem must be solved immediately. Leaders ask themselves: *How bad is it? What is the worst that could happen if this problem is ignored? Does it need to be fixed right away? It seems small, BUT what other things does this impact that could create a bigger issue?* These questions help **put things in perspective**, and may reveal that the problem is not as worrisome as originally thought…or the opposite!

5. Leaders Start By Looking to Themselves for Possible Solutions: If the problem *does* need attention quickly, leaders first look to themselves for answers. They ponder what actions they might take personally that could resolve the problem. They brain-storm all ideas and write them down. If the problem was developed by someone else, they ask that person how *they think* it should be resolved. And if the issue is significant, the leader will go to their team, or trusted advisors, for idea sharing. Being able to get a variety of solutions to choose from, from people with different perspectives and experience, is powerful.

6. Leaders Continually Self-Evaluate: Leaders constantly assess whether the process is going well, if the solutions being discussed make sense, and if they are doing everything they can to solve the issue.

7. Leaders Do Research: Leaders consider what research would be valuable to their problem-solving efforts (like searching the Internet, asking other people, reading books, etc.). Leaders do not think of themselves as all-knowing and understand that the first instinct for an answer is not necessarily the best. And, sometimes when you are too knowledgeable about a subject, you can overlook something obvious.

8. Leaders Make Decisions: Leaders pick a solution and implement it. They may start with a quick-fix solution and follow up with a more long-lasting fix, but they decide what needs to be done...and they do it.

9. Leaders Follow Through: Effective leaders don't just implement the solution and turn away. They follow through with making sure necessary team members are also doing their part (if required). And they ask everyone involved how they think the "solution" is working out now that it's actually being used.

10. A Leader Can 'Let Go': A good leader can let go, but doesn't forget. Harboring the fear, embarrassment, anger, or frustration (whatever emotion the issue evoked) is counter productive, so must be let go. But remembering how it came about, was resolved, and how *you* handled the situation (for future reference), is key.

11. Leaders Create Achievable Markers: Leaders break the problem-solving process into small steps, and then focus on the most immediate steps. They know how to break problems down into their component tasks and then track the progress of each one over measure.

12. Leaders Track Results: Test and monitor any solutions you implement. Don't just assume you're done. Despite your best intentions, any solution you implement might not work; it might even make things worse!

13. Leaders Aren't Too Proud to Say "I'm Wrong": Be ready to undo whatever (ineffective) solution you implemented without shame. A respected leader is never embarrassed to correct mistakes. Without mistakes no progress would ever be made!

Coach Lisa's Comments:

Great leaders do not simply know how to solve problems; *they know how to find them.* They can detect smoke, rather than simply trying to fight raging fires. That's the type of leader I encourage you to be. Have a good rapport with your team, don't make them fearful of you, and encourage them to share bad news, red flags, or concerns with you *quickly*!

And, please note this: I've come across many *ineffective* leaders who try to pass-the-buck by placing the blame on their peers or employees. They act like small children on a playground when confronted by an adult after a toy is broken; all of them point fingers at each other. But when you're a boss and something in your department or team is "broken", and *your supervisor* asks you how or why it happened, you must own it.

You can point fingers at anyone you want, and make up every excuse in the book, but ultimately it's your fault because it happened on your watch. You will do nothing but look foolish in the eyes of your superiors if you sit there placing the blame on everyone else.

Don't be *that* type of leader. You'll lose the respect of your entire team, and the respect of your boss. Take ownership of the issue, respect your team, look for solutions, and solve the problem.

C H A P T E R   T E N

The Ethics of Leadership & 5 Ethical Essentials

Thanks to the broken moral compass of those older than you, in places like Wall Street, corporations, and government, public perception of leadership is at an all-time low. The goal, and this is entirely up to you and your generation, is to be next group of leaders who turn that around. And, again, your effort starts the minute you start working; not after you've reached a senior executive position. Your personal ethics, and your leadership brand with regards to ethics, and how people perceive you as "ethical" or "not-so-ethical", all start forming on Day One at work.

Ethical Questions

At its most basic, **ethics** is about deciding what is right (or *more* right) in a particular situation...determining what ought to be...and deciding what is consistent with one's personal or organizational value system. **Ethical leadership** combines ethical decision-making and ethical behavior, and occurs in both an individual and an organizational context.

The discipline of ethics begins with Socrates' question: *How should one live?* Ethics is about choice. What values guide us? What standards do we use? What principles are at stake? And how do we choose between them? An ethical approach to a problem will inquire about *goals and means* (the instruments we use to achieve these goals) and the *relationship between the two.*

The Values of Ethics

Values exist at the core of human nature; they are the building blocks of our belief system. Ethics are actions that reveal our values within an operating environment. If we say we cherish (value) a clean environment, but continue to pollute (abuse) it, our values and our ethical behavior *are incongruent.* Within a leadership role, the same is true of our attitude toward workers. Recent history of organizational failure underscores how placing **personal greed over expressed organizational values** destroys businesses and, worse, destroys the faith workers have in business leaders. Hello, Enron. Hello, WorldCom.

So today, a major responsibility of a successful business leader must be to make ethical decisions and behave in ethical ways – and to see that the organization **understands and practices its ethical code.**

Sound easy? Unfortunately "temptation" is always around the corner, and has caused some people with a strong moral code to sway and go to the dark side. We see those leaders everyday on the news (priests, politicians, CEO's, cops, etc.), and there are many more we never see but who are getting caught, being fired, and/or going to jail, based on their misconduct.

Greed, fear and *desperation* are individually very powerful emotions that make people do stupid things…but when they are combined, the outcomes can be catastrophic. Example: Wall Street guy gets greedy because he sees what his friends have. He starts doing unethical things to make more money faster. Then he buys

3 houses, 4 cars, etc. And then, when things get tough (like a market shift), he gets scared (*fear*), and *desperate* because he doesn't want to lose everything, and he starts to do things that are even more unethical.

And once you start going down some of these paths, there is no turning back. You're <u>in</u>, regardless of how much guilt you feel or regret you have. Once a line has been crossed, it's either turn yourself in (not necessarily to the cops, but perhaps admitting something to your boss), or keep the façade going.

Ethics Is As Ethics Does

Ethics are the *outward display of values*. When you have clarified *your own personal value system* and have a sense of your organization's values, then ethical behavior for you will be the **actions that are consistent with these values.** Leaders who "walk their talk" and act in accordance with the values they profess, are seen as people of integrity and of strong moral character.

Character is judged, at least partially, on the basis of integrity...and a person's integrity is made *tangible* by their actions!

5 Ethical Essentials Young Leaders Must Embrace:

1. Choose actions that are consistent with 'the road you choose to travel' in your personal life: A clear personal purpose is <u>the foundation for ethical professional behavior</u>.

2. Behave in ways that make you proud: Self-esteem is a powerful tool for behaving ethically. Self-esteem is personal pride mixed with a fair amount of humility, and this balance creates the confidence to "hang tough" when dealing with *ethical dilemmas* (the temptations mentioned earlier).

3. Be patient and have faith in your decisions and yourself:

Patience helps us to behave in ways that will be the best in the long run, thus avoiding the trap of bending your ethics for short-term gain.

4. Behave with persistence: This means behaving ethically all of the time — not just when it is *convenient to do so*. An ethical leader has persistence to stick to his/her purpose to achieve what he/she envisions.

5. Behave in ways that are consistent with what is *really* important: This means keeping perspective. Perspective allows us to reflect and to see things more clearly so that we can see what is really important to guide our behavior.

There's a moral theory called **utilitarianism** which says *the right action is the action that maximizes overall usefulness (utility)*. Utility is how leaders justify bending their ethics and breaking the rules. However, to maintain credibility and inspire follower-ship, leaders cannot make ethical exceptions of themselves.

A Question of Trust

Trust is a key and basic component to any relationship, and trust is in very short supply these days. Many executives and senior leaders are unclear themselves as to their own roles and to their own futures. In the meantime, beneath them (the actual workforce itself), is functioning in a similar atmosphere of fear and powerlessness. They're suspicious of the people above them, creating a "you vs. us" mentality that kills an organization's ability to effectively function.

The study of ethics is a study of humans and human relationships. Ethics define what we should do, and what we should be like as human beings, as members of a group or society, and in the different roles that we play in life...such as our roles in a business setting. Leadership is a particular type of ethical relationship marked by *power and/or influence, vision, obligation, and responsibility.*

By understanding the ethics of the leader-follower relationship, we gain a better understanding of leadership, itself, because some of the central issues in ethics are also the central issues of leadership. They include the personal challenges of authenticity, self-interest, and self-discipline, and moral obligations related to justice, duty, competence, and the greater good.

Ethics are Inspirational

An essential element of leadership is the ability to inspire others to follow by instilling in them optimistic *faith in the competency and ethical "compass" of the person in charge.* Sadly, decades of managerial malfeasance, corporate greed, and the recent economic meltdown has made workers anything but optimistic.

Mistrustful of the ethics and morals of those in charge, 21st Century employees have become jaded and angry towards leadership. In a study conducted by Walker Information, it was found that only about 50% all American working adults believe their senior executives are people of high integrity. It is your job, as our next generation of leaders, to change that!

Can a newly minted supervisor or manager overcome this mistrust? Yes. Young leaders who *identify, articulate, and consistently live up to their values*, are seen as ethical. This turns mistrust into confidence and changes resistant employees into fully committed "partners in success".

Be Seen and Heard

Even in good times, most senior leaders...especially in large organizations...are hardly visible to the rank and file. Tucked away in the executive suites, many leaders are unknown commodities to the people who are expected to follow them. With the exception of an annual corporate function or a disembodied video 'town hall' rah-rah session, leaders can be rarely seen or heard.

Good leaders need to be seen and they need to let their values be heard. During World War II, one of the most effective military leaders was Field Marshall Rommel. One of his key leadership attributes was that he frequently visited, talked and ate with the front line troops. His actions were humanizing, thus making him "one of us" to the troops serving beneath him.

So don't hide in your office or cubicle. Do not be afraid to talk with your staff honestly, alerting them to anticipated changes, and preparing them for continuous, unforeseen challenges, too. Be visible, approachable, and personable, and avoid creating a team where it is "you vs. them".

6 Practical Reasons an Ethical Workplace Matters

Many people are used to reading about or hearing of the **moral benefits** of fostering good business ethics. However, there are other types of benefits, as well, that are tangible, practical, and focused on an organization's success. These include:

1. Attention to business ethics has substantially improved society: Ethical business decisions have led to the abolition of child labor, unfair hiring practices, price fixing, etc. And they have led to the development of oversight groups and regulatory agencies.

2. Ethics help maintain a moral course in turbulent times: During times of change, there is often no clear moral compass to guide leaders through complex conflicts about what is right or wrong. Continuing attention to ethics in the workplace sensitizes leaders and staff to how they want to act – with humanity and for the greater good.

3. Ethics cultivate strong teamwork and productivity: Ongoing attention and dialogue regarding values in the workplace builds openness, integrity and community; critical ingredients of strong teams in the workplace. When employees feel strong alignment between their values and those of their leader and organization, they react with strong loyalty and performance.

4. Ethics support employee growth: Attention to ethics in the workplace helps employees face reality, both good and bad, in the organization and themselves. This provides an opportunity for workers to self-correct and re-align with company values if they (the employee) are starting to behave unethically.

5. Ethics are an insurance policy: Attention to ethics ensures highly ethical policies and procedures in the workplace. It's far better to incur the cost of mechanisms to ensure ethical practices now than to incur costs of litigation later.

6. Ethics promote a strong public image: Attention to ethics is also strong public relations, although certainly ethical behavior should not be done primarily for reasons of public relations. Still, an organization that regularly gives attention to its ethics can portray a strong positive to the public. People see those organizations as valuing people more than profit, and as striving to operate with the utmost of integrity and honor. And that positive image is manifested by the company's leadership and employees, at all levels!

Coach Lisa's Comments:

I think this is one of the most important chapters in the book. Why? Because! Many of the other chapter topics are things that you can learn, and/or become better at, with experience and practice. But your ethics and personal integrity have to come from your personal being.

If your communication skills aren't great, you can work on those. And your boss may mention it to you, but you won't necessarily get in trouble over it (unless you choose not to work on those skills). However, if you do something unethical, even just once, you could not only lose your job, but possibly land in jail. Steal from the company? You could go to jail and ruin your career. Lie to customers for financial gain? You could get fired, and depending on the level of what you've done, possibly go to jail. Sabotage a co-worker for personal gain? This could lead to getting fired and/or ruining your reputation at work.

Basically, anything you choose to do that does not follow a strong code of personal ethics, could become a very big, life altering, negative experience for you. But, it starts with the small stuff: Calling in sick a lot when you're really not; telling little white lies to cover yourself on projects being late; making promises to your team and not keeping them (even if it's promising them something like an off site bowling party, but then never doing it).

Here's a real world example of a young female leader who was faced with a pretty substantial issue. And she shared her story with me, so I'm not making it up just to illustrate a point.

She works for a large company with locations globally, and their headquarters are in the U.S. Her executive supervisors asked her to travel to one of their manufacturing plants in another country just to check in. She was <u>not</u> told there were "issues" at the location and "go fix them". They all actually thought things were going well there, so they simply wanted her to make an appearance on behalf of the U.S. team.

Within a few days of her arrival, she started to see a lot of unethical things going on. These included: People taking vacation time but their bosses not logging it (because their bosses were doing the same thing); shortcuts being taken in the manufacturing process; safety procedures not being followed in the manufacturing plant; and managers and senior executives arranging *personal* kick backs from vendors and customers for their own personal financial gain.

She learned about the kick backs by simply walking around the business offices and hearing phone conversations and people talking amongst each other.

Because this location was performing well, and making money for the company, she could have easily kept her mouth shut to avoid opening a big can of worms that would cause significant mayhem for the organization as a whole. But, her personal ethics and values wouldn't allow her to do that. So when she returned to headquarters, she provided a detailed report, in person, of her findings.

She knew this would be a big deal, and that many people, some of which were senior executives at the other location, would be very angry with her. But she also knew that if she didn't say something, these things would eventually get found out, and her bosses would ask her why she hadn't seen any (or all) of it. Plus, she knew these things were wrong and needed to be fixed.

Within several weeks, many people were fired at that country's location, and new people were hired to fix and maintain policies. And although she did take a lot of heat from some people, her whistle blowing not only resulted in the CEO and senior executives in the U.S. to hold her in a very high regard as a young leader with strong moral character, but she also received a promotion.

I want you to be that type of young leader. I want you to not only walk away from temptations that will compromise your values for (perhaps) financial gain, but to also *not be afraid* of blowing the whistle on people doing thing that are unethical. That is the only way corruption can be reduced, and your generation can lead the change, even just one small step at a time!

C H A P T E R   E L E V E N

41 Expert Leadership Tips: Successful Senior Executives Share Their Advice

A lot of the business events I attend, I'm participating in some way: either as a speaker, panelist, moderator, facilitator, etc. But sometimes I get the pleasure of just "attending" as an audience member, and get to watch everyone else do the work.

FountainBlue presented one such gathering, and it was their monthly "When She Speaks, Women in Leadership Series" event. There were 2 things that motivated me go on that Friday afternoon: The topic for one, plus my friend and colleague, Camille Smith, was moderating the panel. Camille is not only my colleague (we occasionally do presentations together), but she's also my mentor (I call her Yoda), and she's hilarious.

These combined factors got me out of my slippers and sweats, and into my car. And, I can say with total honesty, I was glad I went. So much so, that the main points from that interesting panel prompted me to add this chapter.

I'd like to express special thanks to Linda Holroyd, founder of

FountainBlue (.biz) and the "When She Speaks, Women in Leadership Series". Her hard work has created one of the most prestigious networking associations in the Bay Area. And she graciously granted me permission to use this info for my book.

The panel discussion was entitled: *Leading With Power, Influence and Integrity*. And the panel was comprised of (names of panelists and their companies needed to be withheld based on their employers' legal policies):

Facilitator: Camille Smith, Founder/President, Work In Progress Coaching, Inc.
Panelist: VP of Global Services
Panelist: Principal Scientist (senior executive position)
Panelist: Senior Vice President of HR
Panelist: Senior Director Program Management

Here are 41 of their personal leadership tips and insights they shared that day pertaining to *Leading with Power, Influence and Integrity*:

1. Power, influence and integrity *are three inter-connected circles* that create the foundation for being an effective leader.

2. Whereas there are many ways to describe *power*, the concept of *integrity* is more nebulous. It refers to a concept of wholeness, of alignment with your personal values, as well as that of your organization and your team.

3. Defining leadership moments are not easy. There will be conflict, resistance, difficult circumstances. You may test a relationship, or even jeopardize your job. If you are up to the task and doing the right thing based on your personal

assessment and your personal moral standards, it will prepare you for more of these opportunities to learn and grow and lead.

4. Leading with power, influence and integrity takes the strength and intelligence to make plans and the courage to execute on them, especially under difficult circumstances, especially when many variables impact the right course of action.

5. Leadership goes well beyond positional power, where someone has the authority to manage other people or projects and might rightfully use coercion as a strategy. People can also gain power by becoming an expert/authority on a specific topic, by encouraging/reinforcing others around them.

6. Even if you have positional power, use that power judiciously.

7. Don't be someone you're not. Find your personal "voice" and define your personal brand/style at work.

8. Power is sharing info with people; not withholding it.

9. For every ONE point of "suggestion/constructive criticism" that you offer to an employee, provide NINE compliments.

10. Empowerment and engagement are much more effective at getting things done and building positive relationships.

11. "Power over" is about coercion, being domineering. "Power to" is more about affecting change. "Power with" is

centered on collaboration. "Power Within" is centered on yourself.

12. Be willing to walk away from a company or client without integrity.

13. Never ask anyone to do something you wouldn't personally do.

14. Don't shrink from any conversations with yourself; *you must avoid denial with regards to any situation.* This can lead to small issues becoming huge ones – and people will then be asking you, "How and why did this happen?"

15. Embrace conflict *tactfully*: Speak-up (not in volume, but with opinion), debate with inquiry, and keep inquiring until there is nothing left to say.

16. Communicate with courage and confidence; *not intimidation.*

17. Insist on a seat at the table. Don't avoid *getting involved.*

18. People are listening to what you say...and to what you DON'T say.

19. Be *empathetic* to employee needs and desires.

20. Have your "core values" written down and share them with your team.

21. Be an expert. When faced with something you're not very familiar with, don't fake it. Take the time to research the

topic/issue and get to really understand it. Only then can you be useful in the decision-making process.

22. Proactively manage your relationships with others, AND your relationship with yourself.

23. Power is having information – accurate information about anything. Don't go by rumors. Go to reliable sources and get solid information.

24. Focus on people. They are the most important assets you have.

25. Surround yourself with people who can support you and believe in you…and who are honest with you.

26. Interact with a lot of people at work regularly, and empower people to make decisions versus using your "power card" all the time. The key is to create an "inclusive environment" *versus a dictatorship.*

27. Empower your people; don't "de" power them. This will actually make your life easier.

28. Leadership is not painted in black and white. Be aware of the nuances of behaviors and interactions, and manage accordingly.

29. Be passionate and hold to your true values, your personal moral standards.

30. It may be perceived that adhering to your moral standards would make you *less powerful,* but actually the opposite is

true. When you act with integrity people take notice and give you more power, more influence.

31. Figuring out what's right and wrong might not be as difficult as deciding between two good things.

32. Focus both on your core values and also on the core values of your organization. Ensure alignment when you're considering joining a company, and as you work for a company.

33. Consider strategically who will be impacted by actions and decisions made, and plan accordingly.

34. Be aware that a lot of people are watching what you say and don't say, what you do and don't do. Your next opportunities, and indeed your reputation, will be impacted by the actions and decisions you make day to day, *everyday*.

35. Bring a skill of value to the table.

36. Accept, but manage, your emotions. Most people are less effective at getting things done if too much emotion is distracting them from doing the tasks at hand, or the strategic thinking needed to achieve objectives.

37. Say what you will do, and do what you say you will do.

38. Be the boss you want to have. *Would you want to work for you?*

39. *Leadership is about doing the right thing, even when no one's going to know.* – Oprah Winfrey (a panelist quoted this)

40. *Have the discipline and control to influence your power over others' lives.* – Clint Eastwood (a panelist quoted this)

41. *Know when to hold 'em, know when to fold 'em.* – Kenny Rogers (a panelist quoted this)

Coach Lisa's Comments:

Well, there you go! 41 tips from highly successful, highly respected, senior executives. Each panelist was employed by a different global corporation, and each panelist had 15+ years of workforce experience.

I hope you noticed a few common threads through much of what they shared, such as: respect your employees, lead with integrity and a moral compass, take responsibility for your actions, and learn from everyone & every situation.

Following these tips have worked well for them, so they can work well for you. Many of the tips are also components of developing your personal brand (Tip #7 mentions this). So as you read the next chapter you may want to review the 41 tips a few times in this chapter for some ideas.

Okay! Let's move on to the importance of developing your personal leadership brand, *and how to do it!*

C H A P T E R   T W E L V E

4 Steps to Creating Your Personal Leadership Brand
(and a story about socks)

What is personal branding? Short answer: A strong personal leadership brand allows all that's powerful and effective about your leadership style to become known to your colleagues up, down, and across the organization, thus enabling you to generate maximum value and a unique "distinction" for yourself. Yet while every leader has a brand (either created *by* them, or one created *for* them unknowingly), few methodologies exist to help leaders brand themselves.

But as with product or company branding, if you do not take control of developing and establishing your (personal) brand, and actually put some thought into it versus just letting it happen organically, other people will do it for you…and it may not always be accurate.

This is why many leaders put time and effort into developing their personal brand, and letting it be known. As a young leader, the time to start thinking about and developing your personal brand is now…not after you have been in the workforce for 5-10 years. And, even if you're still in school, the time to start thinking about this is now…it can help you in your job search, finding the right company and/or position that matches your personal brand's values, and can set you apart from the other job seekers out there.

But why do leaders, who are not celebrities, professional athletes, or politicians, go through the trouble of creating a personal brand? Well, let's look at the <u>4 main business benefits of doing it</u>:

Differentiation: A personal brand differentiates you from others – it enables you to stand out among your competition and therefore be more memorable. A leadership brand conveys your identity and distinctiveness as a leader, and it communicates the value you offer to your employees, peers, and supervisors.

Consistency: A personal brand ensures that you are consistent – that is, reliably the same in most situations, which creates trust with key audiences. People know what to expect of you, you communicate from the same platform regardless of circumstance, and it builds a reputation that people will come to rely on.

Clarity: When you have a brand, you stand for something. People around you are clear on your values, and YOU are clear on your values. And as with any brand (personal, product or company), everything you do and decision you make, will start with asking yourself: "If I do this (or act like this, respond like this, say it like this, etc…), will it be supporting, or diluting, and/or mapping to, my personal brand?" You can also see how asking questions like this can help keep your moral compass on the right path!

Authenticity: Lastly, personal branding allows a leader to speak with authenticity. Your personal brand communicates who you really are; not someone you really are not. When a leader's verbal and non verbal communication truly maps to who they are, they are much more persuasive than when they are emulating a fake persona. Remember I mentioned Tip #7 from the executive's in the previous chapter? Here's a reminder: *"Don't be someone you're not. Find your personal 'voice' and define your personal brand/style at work."*

Trying to live life putting up a "front", either in your personal or professional lives, is exhausting. And, btw, most people know when you're doing it…or they eventually always find out. SO JUST BE YOU! You have special traits, values, and strengths to offer the world…and the world will welcome you/them!

Define Your Brand

Start by *defining* your brand, by documenting **the traits that you believe define your leadership style**, using the 6 areas below:

1. **Your Philosophical Style:** Leaders are visionary. They believe in change. They don't ask "Why?" nearly as often as "Why not?"

2. **Your Social Style:** Leaders are listeners. They prefer monologues to dialogues.

3. **Your Intellectual Style:** Leaders need to have enough knowledge to be able to delegate tasks and explore new ways of getting things done.

4. **Your Communication Style:** A leader communicates more

than facts and figures. He/she can communicate passion, excitement, enthusiasm, and/or fun, too.

5. **Your Emotional Style:** Leaders care about other people as well as themselves. They see employees as something more than cogs in the corporate wheel.

6. **Your Ethical Style:** Leaders, through actions and words, create a "safe haven" for growth and development. Their respect for others, and their own personal values, promotes confidence in themselves *and* in others around them...and the most essential component for leadership success? Trust.

4 Steps to Creating a Personal Leadership Brand:

The benefit of consciously shaping a leadership brand is *focus*; when you know with utmost clarity what you want to be known for, and who you *really are*, it is easier to let go of the behaviors, actions, and even projects, that do not let you deliver on your brand *promise*, and to concentrate on ones that do.

Step 1 – Decide What You Wish to Be Known For: Given the context of the business results you want to achieve, consider how you wish to be perceived. Pick any 6 adjectives that describe you, such as: collaborative, independent, results-oriented, calm, fun, driven, supportive, strategic, reliable, compassionate, innovative, etc.

Step 2 – Define Your Identity: The next step is to combine the six adjectives you've listed into (3) two-word phrases that reflect your desired identity. This exercise allows you to build a deeper, more complex description of *not only what you want to be known for, but also how you will probably have to act to get there.* Experimenting with the many combinations that you can make from your six chosen words helps you crystallize your personal leadership brand.

Step 3 – Construct Your Leadership Brand Statement: Words became phrases and now phrases will become a sentence. Plug the phrases you created into the following template and you'll have an 'instant' personal leadership branding statement: **"I want to be known for being _____ so that I can deliver _____."**

An example might be: "I want to be known for being *independently innovative, deliberately collaborative, and strategically results-oriented* so that I can deliver *superior financial outcomes for the company.*"

You can also approach this a bit differently than what was suggested in Step 2. After you have identified several key adjectives, you don't necessarily need to pair them up to make 2-word phrases. You can create your personal branding statement using the formula above but it could be something like: "I want to be known for being *honest, respectful, hard working, collaborative and innovative* so that I can deliver *effective results and solutions for my employer, my team, and my peers.*"

There are many "formulas" (like the one above) out there for creating a personal branding statement. But regardless of the one you choose, the key point is to make sure it's based on your true values, personality, and strengths.

Step 4 – Live Your Brand:
Your personal leadership brand is now complete...or is it? Test it to make certain you can live up to your brand *promise.* Do you

have the ability to translate the qualities you articulate in your leadership brand statement into day-to-day behavior? Can you commit to live the leadership brand you espouse? Can you translate it into the decisions and choices you make?

Pose the following questions to see if it needs to be refined:
- Is this the brand identity that best represents who I am and what I can do?
- If I "live" this declaration of leadership, will I consider myself a success?
- Am I willing to tell others that this is my personal leadership brand?
- Is this brand identity something that creates value in the eyes of my organization and key stakeholders?
- Is this brand true to who I am?

This last question is an important one...and the answer can be a trap for many would-be leaders. It can be tempting to choose a brand identity that supports organizational values, but not your own personal values and strengths. Some people believe that a *company-focused* personal leadership brand will make them seem more valuable to the organization. But this premise is wrong.

Your personal brand statement and brand promise must be true to who you are; not about what your employer may want to hear. And your personal brand statement is something that you can *take with you* to a new company or position, and have it still be accurate. It's about who you are as a person and leader; not who you believe *a company* wants you to be. If you follow that silly path, you'll be changing "who you are" (your brand) every time you get a new job. That's ridiculous.

Bonus Tips from Dan Schawbel, Personal Branding Expert

Dan Schawbel, author of *Me 2.0*, has recently been called "a leading voice in the area of personal branding" by major media. He graduated college in 2006 and sees the branding world as it is, not as it was. And his book is a valuable primer for achieving a competitive edge, using the tools and techniques of the 21st Century.

Dan describes branding as a journey of discovery. As you work to brand yourself, you will discover the attributes that make you who you are. He recommends using unique life experiences – personal and professional – to set yourself apart from the crowd.

To achieve this, Dan recommends you ask (and answer!) the following 5 questions:

1. What makes me special?
2. What do people in my 'network' think is special about me?
3. Have I ever been complimented for a particular skill or talent?
4. Is there something I do well and am passionate about?
5. What achievements in my life am I most proud of?

And for Millennial job seekers looking to establish a positive brand to attract employment opportunities, he also recommends that you create a **Personal Branding Toolkit** with the following:

1. Resume – With sections devoted to objective, summary, education, technical skills, work experience, and extracurricular activities. And it can be profiled on business sites like LinkedIn or social sites like Facebook.

2. Portfolio – An opportunity to display your best work in print, on a CD, or on your website.

3. Website – Create your own online presence that is engaging, user-friendly and easy to navigate. It should include your name, picture, and personal branding statement.

4. Blog – Use these new channels of communication as great platforms for self-promotion. Use yours to post content that is original, appealing, informative, and (this is the key) likely to generate responses, and attract employment opportunities in your chosen field.

5. Avatar – Pictures speak volumes. An 'avatar' is the small picture that you create to represent yourself on social networking sites. Using a self-portrait instead of an icon will help people associate your writing and your online presence *with you.*

Tip from Coach Lisa: Make your blog, vidcast, podcast, etc. about the <u>industry</u> *you're targeting for employment! It can attract companies to you, and will keep you current on industry news while you're unemployed, plus will impress employers in interviews when you tell them about your industry-focused blog (or Twitter presence or whatever social media tool you choose). And make sure the url(s) are on your resume and cover letter!*

Lisa's Coaching Comments:

The concept of developing a personal brand at work is not new, but it's starting to be discussed and written about a lot more. We all know celebrities have been doing it forever. And although all of us non-celebs have been doing it forever, too (either knowingly or not), it's something now that is becoming a key component of management and leadership training. Companies, coaches and consultants are working more and more with employees to help them better understand who they are, what they stand for, and how they want to be perceived.

I know senior executives who post their personal branding statement on a wall in their office because they want everyone to know what they stand for. And they require their employees to create one for themselves. It can not only help individuals get clarity but can also create clarity within a team…everyone becomes clear on the values and strengths of their team members.

As a young leader, this is something you can consider doing with your team. Yes, create your own personal branding statement, but have your employees create theirs, too, and then everyone can share them in a group setting. It's an effective, fun activity, and can really open up some interesting, useful dialogue between your team members, foster team building, and improve understanding of each other.

One other thing I wanted to add about building your personal branding…part of the process can also include "visual" branding. An example of this is Larry King's suspenders, Don King's and Donald Trump's wacky hair styles, or Ellen DeGeneres always wearing sneakers. All of these visual things are part of their "overall" brand identities.

Here's the sock story: I know a young Millennial woman who was an engineer at a large corporation. Aside from standing out as a woman (because of all the male engineers), she wanted something more that reflected her personal brand (one of her values being "have fun at work"). So she started to wear wild socks to work with her nice business attire. Now people bring her hilarious, weird socks at work. And one day she was walking down the hall, and the CEO of the company (whom she had never met) stopped her and said "Hey, you're the engineer who wears weird socks. Which ones do you have on today?"

Yes, of course, she is respected for her intelligence and work ethic, but now even the CEO of a company with 10,000+ employees knows who she is, AND has her on his radar. He actually stops her now every time he sees her on campus and asks her to show her socks to him (and whoever he is with…typically other senior execs). Plus, he's brought her up on stage at large company events to show her socks, and he has asked her to be on special project teams!

Just by her taking the time to develop her personal branding statement, she was able to think of a "visual" aspect to support it and standout, and now senior executives all over the company know her...and it all started with her socks.

PART THREE

Key Components for Successfully Building & Retaining Your Team

"In the end, all business operations can be reduced to three words: people, product and profits. Unless you've got a good team, you can't do much with the other two."

– Lee Iacocca
World Renowned Businessman, Philanthropist and
Voted 18th Greatest CEO of All Time

INTRODUCTION TO PART THREE

Key Components for Successfully Building & Retaining Your Team

So far in this book we've covered a lot of ground to help you understand what leadership is, how to become an effective leader, how to develop your personal leadership brand & style, and a variety of other things. But now we're going to jump into how you can create, develop, manage, and retain a top-notch team. This is key for becoming an effective, successful, young leader!

I have mentioned many times so far that your people are your biggest "asset". But unfortunately many managers, senior executives, and companies don't follow that way of thinking. They look at employees as commodities that can easily be disposed of and replaced. As a young leader, having that type of philosophy is the kiss of death for your success. You are truly only as good as the people you surround yourself with, so if you can't successfully recruit, manage and retain good people, you are only hurting yourself. And, eventually, you'll be the one who is fired...or if you own a business, lose it.

Okay! No need for a longer intro than that…let's dive into Part Three!

CHAPTER   THIRTEEN

33 Strategies for Identifying and Hiring a Top Team...*Plus Tips for Termination When Someone's Gotta Go!*

Staffing-up is particularly challenging for new managers who may find themselves on the hiring side of the table for the first time in their careers. The process is both an art and a science that continues to evolve. Still, there are some basic "best practices" that can be followed to make identifying and hiring talent more effective, and we'll be covering those in a minute.

As a young leader, it's important that you realize the most important aspect of any business is **recruiting, selecting, and retaining** top people. Research shows those organizations that spend more time recruiting high-caliber people earn **22% higher return** to shareholders than their industry peers. However, many companies rely on outdated and ineffective interviewing and hiring techniques, and they *don't train their young leaders on how to do this effectively.*

But by following these tips, you can put yourself ahead of the game, early in your career, and create a winning team!

6 Tips to Identify the Best Person for the Job

Every employer is eager to hire a competent person to complement his/her team. Generally, they are looking for someone with superior professional skill, good deportment and winning ways with people. But finding the combination of *competence, personal presence and charisma* is not always easy to identify. And although there are no guarantees, there are a few steps you may consider to maximize your efforts to find just the "right" people you need.

Tip #1 – Create a Position Description: Many prospective employers like to think that they know what they want. But, when confronted with a variety of talented candidates, they seldom know which particular skills they are focusing on. So writing a **position description** can be helpful because it will make you focus on skills, experience and professional qualities likely to make an employee succeed in the role you want to fill. This may sound like *common sense*, but unfortunately it is not *common practice*!

Tip #2 – Prioritize Your Needs: The position description will only define a set of *minimum competencies*. It will never adequately define the "perfect person" you really seek. There are additional questions that you must ask to help you see the skills that you need more clearly. These questions will also help you to eliminate candidates with talent not relevant to your most immediate needs:

- Which experiences are most relevant?
- If forced to make a choice, which qualities am I willing to forego?
- If I have to leave 1-2 things off my wish-list, what would they be?

Tip #3 – Create A Wish List: If someone is currently acting in, or temporarily assuming, the role you want to fill, another approach is to list his/her professional qualities and then to *add the ones you would like to see in a new hire for that role.* This is often a useful way to critically assess the role itself and your needs for filling it with the right person.

Tip #4 – Model on Success: Another effective approach is to identify another employee you have (or co-worker you know) who comes closest to what you want and, again, list his/her attributes and qualifications as a "template/guide". The point here is to develop a concrete model of the kind of candidate you would like to attract to the role.

Tip #5 – Know How Much You Are Willing To Pay: The truth is that the market has probably defined a compensation range for the talent you seek, so do some research. Then, if you have the means, increase the salary a bit and enhance the benefits package so that you are more likely to attract talent of the highest caliber. And, please note, it is always smart to negotiate from a position of knowledge. So do your homework!

Tip #6 – Use Your Networks to Identify Talent: As you are doing your research to find out which salaries and packages might work for the employee you seek, take time to ask your network about the outstanding candidates they know. Call up those candidates and find out if they might be interested. And even if they're not, find out what kinds of packages they would find attractive *if they were seeking a new job.* This will serve two purposes: it will spread the word that you are looking (within a well-defined, high-integrity network), and it will give you more valuable information about market expectations.

6 Tips for Conducting a Productive Interview

The main purpose of a job interview is to *get information*. Unfortunately, many interviews become an uncomfortable face off between an interviewer behind a desk and a nervous applicant. The key to successful discussions, in which both sides open up and talk candidly, is *helping candidates relax and then drawing them out*. To make the interview more relaxed and productive from the start, consider these ideas:

1. Step out from behind your desk.

2. The seating arrangement should make you and the candidate equals.

3. Offer the candidate something to drink, and if they do, then pour it, or get it, yourself. This simple gesture will make it clear you aren't some young leader on a power trip.

4. Lead in with a little idle conversation and tell candidates about your company. It's also a good idea to add a little of your background into the mix (offering things like: where you came from, why you were attracted to the company, why you like working there, etc.).

5. Phrase questions carefully: The way you phrase a question can make a person either tense up or relax. Instead of asking, "What are your major strengths and weaknesses?" consider asking, "What do you like most about what you do?" or "Tell me about the best days on your current (or most recent) job and then about your toughest days?"

6. Pay attention to the questions *candidates* ask. When they ask things like, "How quickly will I be trained?" or "How much responsibility will I have?" those can be indications that the candidate will be a go-getter. If they spend a lot of time asking about how stressful the job is, how many hours they are expected to work, vacation policies, etc., you may be interviewing someone who won't have the "drive and work ethic" you are seeking.

11 Tips for Getting the Answers You Need

Again, your main objective is to find out as much as you can about the individual you are meeting with. However, you must refrain from making this an interrogation. So after you've established some rapport and put the candidate at ease, you can then move into the interview process with specific questions.

To maximize your fact-finding expedition, you'll need to ask questions that explore a wide range of hard skills (i.e. proficiency with a specific computer program) and soft skills (i.e. aptitude for dealing with others). The sample questions below are probing, but perfectly legal to ask a candidate and will give you some good insight into the person.

It is NOT intended that all questions and categories be addressed with a candidate. Choose only what is relevant to the position you are trying to fill.

Tip #1 – Ask Coping Questions: These questions reveal whether the candidate can maintain a mature, problem solving attitude while dealing with interpersonal conflict, rejection, hostility or time demands:

- Tell me about a time when you had to cope with strict deadlines or time demands. Give me an example.
- Give me an example of a time at work when you had to deal with unreasonable expectations of you.
- When have you had to cope with the anger or hostility of another person? Give me an example.
- Sooner or later we all deal with interpersonal conflict or personal rejection at work. Give me an example of a time when you had to cope with these and how you handled it.
- Tell me about a high stress situation when it was hard for you to keep a positive attitude (but you managed to). What happened?

Tip #2 – Ask Tolerance Questions: These questions can give you insights into whether the candidate is able to withhold actions or speech in the absence of all necessary information, deal with unresolved situations, or can cope with frequent changes, delays or unexpected events:

- When have you been most proud of your ability to wait for important information before taking action in solving a problem? How did the wait affect you?
- People differ in their preference of job duties and work cultures. Some desire structure and very little "surprises", and others thrive on frequently changing environments. Tell me about a time when you were successful in dealing with a (fairly) unstructured, fast moving, work environment. How did you feel and handle it? Ask the same types of questions but regarding a <u>highly structured</u> environment.
- What has been your experience in working with conflicting, delayed or ambiguous information? What did you do to make the most of the situation?

Tip #3 – Ask Decisiveness Questions: The following questions can help reveal whether the candidate is able to make decisions quickly and take action effectively:

- Describe an unexpected situation in which you had to draw a conclusion quickly and take speedy action. What was the outcome?
- Tell me about a situation when you had to stand up for an idea you had, or decision you made, even though it wasn't necessarily popular with your co-workers.
- Give me an example of a situation in which you were especially skillful in making a decision quickly. What was the outcome?

Tip #4 – Ask Spoken Communication Questions: These questions can determine whether the candidate is able to clearly present information, influence or persuade others through oral presentation (in positive or negative circumstances), and listen well:

- What has been your experience in giving explanations or instructions to others?
- What types of experiences have you had in talking with customers or clients?
- Tell me about a time when you had to communicate under difficult circumstances.
- Tell me about an experience of yours that illustrates your ability to influence another person verbally.
- Tell me about a time when your *ability to listen* helped you communicate better.

Tip #5 – Ask 'Energy' Questions: Ask these to help you determine if the candidate is able to create positive energy (motivation) in both individuals and groups:

- Give me an example of a time when your positive attitude caused others to be motivated or energized.
- Give me an example of something you did which helped build enthusiasm in others.
- Tell me about a time you were able to use: A. Competition B. Recognition and C. Reward to encourage others, and that created a positive outcome.

Tip #6 – Ask Policy and Procedural Questions: Here are a few questions that can reveal whether the candidate is able to handle and conform to (existing/established) routine operations, solutions, policies and procedures:

- Tell me about your experiences in logging (documenting) your work activities in a required format/process. Be specific.

- Select a job you have had and describe the paper-work/projects/processes you were required to complete. What specific things did you do to insure your accuracy?
- Give me an example of a time when you found or created a systematic method for solving work problems (or improving a process).
- Tell me about a time when you found that an established method of doing something was ineffective, or could be modified to be better. What did you do about it? Did you share your opinion/solution with a supervisor?

Tip #7 – Ask Analytical Problem-Solving Questions: These questions reveal whether the candidate is able to use a systematic approach in solving problems through the analysis of problems, and evaluation of alternate solutions:

- Tell me about a time when you were systematic in identifying potential problems at work. Feel free to showcase your analytical skills.
- What was your greatest success in using principles of logic to solve technical problems at work?
- Give me an example of a time when you actively defined several solutions to a single problem. Did you use tools such as research, brainstorming with others, etc.?

Tip #8 – Ask Goal-Setting Questions: Ask these to find out whether the candidate is able to define realistic, specific goals and objectives:

- What have been your experiences with defining long-term goals? Tell me 1-2 specific goals you set and how successful were you at achieving it?
- Give me an example of a time you used a systematic process to define your objectives.

- Goal statements are often made to meet the expectations of others. Tell me about a time when you took the initiative to set goals and objectives yourself, even though you weren't directed to do so by someone else.

Tip #9 – Ask Commitment to Task Questions: These questions can tell you whether the candidate is able to start, and persist, with specific courses of action:

- Give an example of any specific time in which you found it necessary to give long hours to a job.
- Tell me about a time when you were able to provide your own motivation to push through a difficult task/project, even though you were working alone. How did you do it?
- Do you have a strong sense of urgency about getting short term results? Or do you have a more laid back approach to work? Give an example.
- Being successful takes more than luck. Tell me about a time when you had to work very hard to reach a goal(s). Be specific about what you achieved.

Tip #10 – Ask Interaction Questions: These questions can reveal whether the candidate is able to communicate with others effectively:

- Describe a time when you were able to be personally supportive and reassuring to a colleague in need.
- Being skillful in dealing with other people on the job is an important factor in being productive. Describe a time when you were successful in dealing with a co-worker you may have had "struggled" with, but were able to get past that and build a nice relationship with them.
- Describe a time when you made a special effort to treat another person in a way which showed your respect for the other person's feelings.

Tip #11 – Avoid Illegal Questions: Federal and State laws prohibit asking certain questions during an interview. The bottom line is that you are forbidden from discriminating against any person on the basis of gender, age, race, national origin, religion or disabilities. If you have any concern that a question you are about to ask may be construed as discriminatory, don't ask it. And to really cover yourself in an effort to avoid a law suit (for you or the company), run any questions you plan to ask in an interview by someone in your HR department (or the equivalent in your company):

- You cannot ask about a person's church, synagogue or parish, or the religious holidays they observe, or their political beliefs. However, while it is *illegal* to ask, "Does your religion allow you to work on Saturdays?" it is acceptable to ask this question, "This job requires occasional work on Saturdays. Is that a problem?"

- You may not ask about native language, the language a candidate speaks at home, or how they acquired the ability to read, write or speak a foreign language.

- You cannot ask about ancestry, national origin, parentage, or birthplace, but you can ask whether they are a U.S. Citizen or a resident alien with the right to work in the U.S.

- You cannot ask about a candidate's age, date of birth, or the ages of their children. However, if their appearance seems questionable (they look *really* young), you can ask whether they are over 18 years old.

Note: *There are also some very good, inexpensive, online assessment tools that you can have job candidates take as part of your interviewing process. Some larger companies utilize these, but many companies do not. There are many different types of hiring/talent assessment tools, and they can help you determine*

strengths, values, traits, skills, etc. in the top candidates you iden-
tify. Thus, moving you closer to finding the right person(s), faster.

10 Tips for Terminating an Employee

As a young leader, you are going to be faced with firing people. And I'm sure there are many of you reading this that have not yet dealt with this task. Typically, it's never easy. Even if you are thrilled that you get to boot someone who has caused you nothing but stress, it can still be really uncomfortable.

I've seen many leaders keep a "less than desirable" employee around WAY longer than they should have because they simply didn't want to deal with the discomfort of firing them (and they just kept hoping things would get better). But, I will tell you this from my personal experience as a 20-year business owner: Under-performing employees don't just drop the ball in regards to their own tasks. *They can trigger a ripple effect of negativity that spreads out to infect everyone and everything around them.* They can create enormous resentment within your organization, which can keep an entire team, department, or company from living up to its full potential.

That said, here are some tips you can follow when getting ready to fire someone. And, again, I recommend getting someone from HR in-the-loop as soon as possible (like right when you start to even "think" this person may be an issue). There are many laws that protect employees for wrongful termination, even if they were rotten employees, so make sure you do everything correctly, so that you and/or your company don't get sued.

1. Give Fair Warning: All performance-based firings should begin with a warning or probationary period. If you let employees know they're on the bubble, they just might turn things around. And if they've put in years of service, it's the least they deserve. "Non performance firings" (based on something like stealing or inappropriate behavior) typically don't require warnings and can be immediate. But make sure you have run your reason by someone in HR first, and request your boss or someone from HR is present when the person is confronted and terminated. Regardless of why they are being terminated, you need to make sure the process is done correctly and by-the-book.

2. Document Everything: Once you've told an employee he/she is on probation, document every task and interaction. The better records you keep, the easier it will be to *justify your actions* should termination be required, or if you find yourself defending your reasons in legal proceedings.

3. Timing is Everything: Most experts agree to fire people early in the day and early in the week. The worst time to terminate an employee is the day before a weekend or holiday.

4. Have Your Paperwork Ready: Don't wait until after you fire an employee to deliver termination paperwork. Pay, including any benefits and unused vacation, is required to be given to them on the spot. HR will make sure this is done correctly (or seek outside professional counsel if your company doesn't have an HR department/employee).

5. Don't Go It Alone: Including a representative from the HR department in a termination meeting adds a sense of gravity and finality to the conversation. And if the employee asks a policy question you can't answer, your expert is right there. It also provides a witness on your side should you end up in court.

6. Keep Things Private: Reassure the employee that the details of the termination are strictly confidential...and then make sure they are.

7. Don't Drag It Out: Say what you have to say, say it clearly and don't say any more. Prolonging the firing meeting allows the employee to start believing he/she is involved in a negotiation, and that they have a chance to talk their way back into the job. Plus, the longer the meeting, the more chance for emotions (on both sides) to ignite.

8. Choose Your Words and Your Tone With Care: In a termination, *how* you say what you have to say is almost as important as the substance of your comments. Be sure to convey a tone of cordiality and civility; even sympathy if you do feel compassion towards the person. As a leader, you could be faced with firing people whom you really like; they just weren't right for the job. And, you will even be asked by superiors to fire people that you don't think should be fired. But regardless of the circumstances, if you are compassionate towards the person, you also need to remain "firm" in your approach and delivery. Again, even if you adore this person, they cannot feel that this is a "negotiation" for keeping their job.

9. Allow Feedback: It may be difficult, but you should encourage the employee to voice his/her feelings after the news has been delivered. If their emotions start to turn ugly, however, take charge and cut the discussion short. Remember that you're terminating an employee, not engaging in a dialogue (or a debate). BTW: This is a really good scenario for using the 80/20 rule I discussed in Chapter 8 (let them do most of the talking…and sit quietly!).

10. If Possible, End on a High Note: Always offer words of encouragement and confidence regarding the employee's future career. Be courteous and respectful. Stand and extend your hand to indicate the meeting has ended. And of course, thank the employee for his/her service.

Coach Lisa's Comments:

I've already expressed several times in this book that your people are your biggest asset. So I don't need to drill the point deeper again now. And the tips provided for interviewing and assessing a candidate are all pretty self-explanatory. But I would like to share one real world example that illustrates the importance of listening to an employee who has an issue with another employee, and they have come to you with their complaint.

I spoke to a young manager who had a female employee tell him she was being sexually harassed by a male co-worker. The young manager shared this information with the big boss of their department. The big boss thought the female employee who was complaining was overreacting, so advised the young manager not do anything about the situation. However, the young manager agreed with the female employee, but because the young manager was intimidated by his boss, he took this advice and did nothing.

The sexual harassment occurred again, and the victim took it upon herself to get legal counsel and sued the company for not helping her, and she won the case. This also led to not only the young manager being fired, but his big boss and the co-worker who did the harassing, were also terminated.

Heed this advice as a young leader: If you feel that a situation could (even remotely) warrant firing someone or giving them a written warning, but your supervisor doesn't agree with your opinion, go over her/his head to someone else for advice. Not all supervisors you work for are going to know the "laws" about work-force issues pertaining to termination, and their personal opinions could be wrong. Seek advice from HR, and if they're not sure, they will know to seek legal advice. Don't potentially lose your job, or get your company into legal trouble, just because you are intimidated by your boss! Go with your gut, and/or personal values and opinions, and get guidance from people inside or outside of your company who are qualified.

CHAPTER   FOURTEEN

10 Ideas to Increase Retention by Rewarding (Groups & Individuals)

It is a common belief that competitors present the biggest threat to business success. The fact is that a threat that exists *within* a company itself trumps any outside forces. And what is one of the biggest threats your company or department may face, and that you may have to deal with as a young leader? Unhappy employees.

Workers who have become disenchanted with their jobs can create havoc in a company with internal sabotage, large and small. They can also quit and take company secrets with them...possibly to your competition or to become competitors themselves. The best way to combat this internal threat is with strategies to keep the best and brightest among your employees satisfied.

Thus, focusing on employee rewards and recognition may be the wisest business decisions any company, and young leader, can make. Do you know that the number one reason a person leaves a job is due to lack of rewards & recognition? Sure, pay, benefits, job satisfaction, etc. are all in the Top Ten reasons, but on average lack of rewards & recognition rank the highest. When a person doesn't feel appreciated and valued, they eventually leave to go somewhere they do.

Ask bosses what makes employees happy at work, and many are likely to think in terms of tangible rewards: a good salary, a pleasant office, generous benefits. Ask employees themselves, however, and increasingly the "happiness factor" depends heavily on intangibles, such as *respect, trust, and fairness.*

But when focusing on rewards such as bonuses, recognition ceremonies, etc., it is wise to remember that a fundamental truth about employee retention is that employees who are satisfied with their work *and with their immediate supervisor* are more likely to classify themselves as "happy" and less likely to jump ship...*regardless of compensation.*

And it's important to note that particular forms of compensation "rewards" come and go with the times. Stock options had great cachet in the 1990s until the bubble burst. And filling retirement funds with company stock seemed great until Enron and others went bust.

So it's important to understand that the *value* of rewards must be judged by a different standard. This has special significance in today's multi-generational workforce. As a young leader, it's imperative to understand, that to be effective, a reward must be tailored to be meaningful to the recipient. But what does that mean?

It means that a one-size-fits-all rewards system isn't effective. What you might perceive as a great reward, someone else may not. That is why it's so important that you truly get to know each of your employees as individuals, and learn what excites and motivates each one of them.

Your company may already have a set rewards program in place, but that doesn't mean you can't create your own ideas for your team, too. And if your company does not have a rewards program in place, then you really need to create one for your group.

Reward Your Team!

The subject of employee rewards has been studied in great detail and a library of literature exists on the subject. One of the best examples is Bob Nelson's "1001 Ways to Reward Employees". I strongly recommend that you pick up a copy! In it, he mentions the advantages of *creating employees who are so filled with an internal fire for success that managers and supervisors don't have to constantly light a fire under them.*

Yet, somehow, it doesn't come so easily for most managers, leaders and organizations. Many can't figure out the right ingredients for job satisfaction, thus leading to higher turnover and unrealized productivity potential. For other companies, creating a rewards program (or just fostering a rewards *culture*) seems expensive and difficult to directly connect to bottom-line results.

For years, employers focused on handing out perks such as pay raises, performance bonuses, extra vacation time, and even preferential treatment (i.e. the coveted corner office or weekend at the company condo). These motivators aren't necessarily bad ideas, but are rather *short-term solutions* that inevitably lead to an eventual drop in performance again. After all, how motivating is a bonus check or vacation that's eight months away? For many people, not very!

Again, this is all about making your employees feel valued and respected, often. So to only express your happiness and appreciation for them once a year (with a trip or bonus check), or during their "required" quarterly or bi-annual review, isn't often enough!

Two decades of research tells us that dangling carrots like this can't create a sustained shift in employee engagement and productivity. So what can? *Consistently* rewarding employees, and sincerely expressing your gratitude and appreciation!

Understanding *what* rewards motivate your team members is essential to being a successful young leader, but you must also know *how* to give it to them; and that takes both will and skill. Quite honestly, most managers are uncomfortable handing out praise, and even just saying "Thank you" to their team members.

Luckily, the reality is that employee rewards are cost-effective and easy to implement on a daily basis. Plus, low-cost and no-cost rewards deliver a tremendous ROI with regard to employee satisfaction, and that translates into productivity and retention.

Let's now jump into 9 ideas you can easily implement. And, as I mentioned before, pick up a book or 2 that offer tons of ideas. You're sure to find a few strategies that work really well for you!

10 Ideas to Increase Retention by Rewarding (Groups & Individuals):

So, what rewards do matter to employees? Well, the best place to start is to ask your employees directly how they would like to be recognized and rewarded. The insights they provide may open your eyes to a variety of opportunities available and enable you to more effectively demonstrate that you appreciate their contributions to the workplace.

But to get your creativity bubbling, here are some popular ideas other companies and managers use to recognize and reward their employees:

Reward #1 – Letters of Acknowledgement: A formal, informal, or semi-formal employee recognition letter works wonders. A message that points to specific contributions the employee made (related to a project or situation) goes a long way in helping employees feel recognized and rewarded. In fact, a semi-formal employee recognition letter that includes a bonus check or a gift card (for a place or product you *know they like*; not something you "think" they like) magnifies the recognition an employee experiences.

Reward #2 – Autonomy: Give employees the freedom to move around within their position, without sacrificing job performance. Employees who feel some ownership over their positions care more about what they do and feel more responsible for its success.

- Give employees the freedom to work independently (not micromanaged)
- Give employees flexibility in work hours (where position allows)
- Allow individuals to develop/improve processes for accomplishing tasks (where appropriate)

Reward #3 – Professional Development/Advancement: Having knowledgeable and competent employees is key to success. Providing them with the tools and opportunities to increase and hone their skills gives you a more qualified staff to work with.

- Allow staff to take advantage of formal training opportunities
- Allow staff to utilize the new skills they learn as soon as possible
- Give employees the opportunity to brief others on what they learned in training
- Provide in-house training and cross-training opportunities

Reward #4 – Fun: Doing something fun once in a while allows employees to let go of the stresses of the day (week or month) and re-energize themselves to be more productive! This can also create better relationships within the office if employees are allowed to "goof around" with their work mates. Other *fun* things include:

- Write positive comments on Post-It notes and leave them for employees to find
- Give team members Silly String to let off a little steam during high stress times
- Provide opportunities to laugh and socialize
- Throw lunch parties to celebrate special events

Reward #5 – Provide Meaningful Work: There are tasks to everyone's job that are less enjoyable than others, but there may be opportunities to assign work that is challenging, fun and/or meaningful to the employee and that furthers the department in reaching their goals. Of course, the less enjoyable tasks must still be done, but providing opportunities for a variety of tasks may enhance the job enough to make those "other" duties less tedious.

- Recognize individual talents and interests when assigning work projects
- Let staff cross train on other functions
- Allow for some variety of job duties which may break up the monotony
- Rotate interesting projects among employees
- Ask employees what else they'd like to be doing/trying to be more satisfied at work

Reward #6 – Empowerment: Employees don't necessarily want to *run* the department, but they may like to contribute to "bettering" the department. This makes them feel a part of something and that their opinions matter. You, as their manager, or other supervisors, will make the final decision, but employee insights may help broaden your perspective, too.

- Ask staff directly for their opinions and ideas (individually and in meetings)

- Encourage them to provide you feedback at any time
- Have staff participate on committees and in meetings
- Recommend your employees to others as a resource or subject matter expert
- Assign staff projects which draw on employees' ideas and creativity

Reward #7 – Prizes: Little prizes can go a long way in saying "thanks" even if the monetary value is not high. Be creative and customize the prizes that you are giving to the employee that you are giving it to. This lets your employees know that you recognize and appreciate their work and that you are interested in them as individuals. Prizes can be given for completing special projects, making significant departmental improvements & contributions, reaching goals and other noteworthy accomplishments.

- Gift certificates (cannot be redeemable for cash)
- Candy Bars (inexpensive, yet appreciated)
- Concert tickets to see someone you know they love

Reward #8 – Recognition: Employees should know how much their work is being valued – by their supervisor and by their department. While recognition need not be done by means of a lavish ceremony, it should be done quickly and clearly. Employees should know what they are being recognized for and be encouraged to continue contributing in a positive way.

- Hold special meetings regularly to celebrate successes and special events (Service Awards, special accomplishment awards, etc.)
- Create a "Thank You" board where *employees* can post thank you notes *for other employees* (i.e.: Mike! Thanks for staying late last night with me to get the project done!)
- Name a space in a department after an employee and put up a sign

- Develop your own departmental award program and create a certificate/trophy. *Example: One manager bought a $2 plate, painted it gold, wrote a silly award name on it, and people vie to get that plate all the time. To have it on your desk has become a "big deal" in their department with a lot of meaning.*

Reward #9 – Time Off: Many people would appreciate an unexpected "Great job! Take Monday off!" type of reward (versus a small bonus check or gift card). We all like time off! And it's easy to implement and much appreciated!

Reward #10 – Commemorative Gifts: These are *small tokens* that you can give to your employees that will recognize the things that they have done for you. This is different than giving them a monetary bonus, because it is actually giving them something that they can *display and be proud of.* Things along these lines are: *Good quality* engraved plaques, pens, watches, desk clocks, etc. And I'm not referring to tacky promotional items with your company logo all over it; I'm referring to items of good quality that you can personalize for each person.

Coach Lisa's Comments:

According to their website, one of the most frequently asked question put to the Society of Human Resource Management is: *"How do we keep talent from jumping to our competitors?"*

Now, combine that question with a popular saying that I mentioned before: *"People don't leave their companies; they leave their managers".*

See? The pressure on you to be an effective young leader, and continue to grow into an effective older leader, is huge. Companies that can retain the best talent, the longest, at any position level, will do the best. And, although many companies offer terrific *company-*

wide policies, perks and reward programs, the power of those things wear off quickly if someone is stuck with a manager they don't like, and/or who never expresses gratitude. Things like benefits, company cars, stock options, expense accounts, travel, interesting work, company parties, room for advancement, etc. ALL become meaningless (after a period of time) if the person's day-to-day manager is a chump. And being unappreciative, or being **unable to express gratitude and kudos**, are typically the leading "chump" qualities.

Here's the deal: It used to be that strong leadership meant the ability to motivate employees. But the reality is that most employees are motivated and want to do a great job; it is **work environments that de-motivate** them. When managers consistently fail to provide the direction, resources, respect and recognition that employees require, their **innate desire to achieve** mutates and becomes re-directed (typically to another job).

Throughout this book I've shared tips and strategies that can help you manage and lead people effectively, such as: communication strategies, attributes of effective leaders, tips from leaders on how to be one, problem solving strategies, building your personal leadership brand, and tons of other useful info sprinkled throughout.

But, not much of those insights matter much if you can't retain your employees! And, as I mentioned earlier, a leading reason people leave their jobs is due to lack of (regular/frequent) recognition. And the responsibility of that falls on you as a leader. So make your people feel appreciated and respected on a regular basis (not just at the required "employee review" time), and you have a very good chance of experiencing a low turnover rate…and creating a very loyal team.

CHAPTER   FIFTEEN

What Young Leaders Need to Know About Employee Engagement

Courtesy of Sara Roberts, President & CEO of Roberts Golden Consulting

Getting into college isn't want it used to be. Students were judged on their SAT scores and their grades, period.

Today, high school students are expected to show leadership skills, to participate in multiple extracurricular activities, contribute to society by working in community betterment activities, have a commitment to the environment, and, oh, yes, excel in grades and in their SAT scores.

Across time, we've come to know Baby Boomers, Gen Jones, Gen X and the Millennials. And there tends to be a wide gulley between mindsets.

Values, experience, and job satisfaction vary widely between Millennials and their older cultural cousins. But with all the differences and all those changes there is one unalterable truth: Employee engagement transcends.

So what *is* employee engagement? It's a heightened emotional connection that an employee feels for his or her organization. And that feeling influences him or her to exert greater effort at work.

But here's the unfortunate truth: Some organizations have the gift of taking committed, enthusiastic people and turning them into cynics over time. This statement rings true for too many companies, despite good intentions.

While today's bottom-line-oriented business environment demands that business owners, executives, and managers keep a close eye on costs, they miss the opportunity to strengthen their profit potential through strong efforts to engage employees.

Now: Throw away your magic wand because engagement isn't easy to acquire. It rests upon a genuine commitment by everyone from executive management to line-level employees. Getting everyone on the same page is certainly a challenge. The key drivers of engagement are:

1. Trust and integrity
2. Nature of the job
3. Line of sight between employee performance and company performance
4. Career growth opportunities
5. Coworkers/team members
6. Employee development
7. Relationship with one's manager.

Perhaps these sound a bit lofty, or even one-sided. Some might say it's certainly not a way to run a company. But the numbers don't lie. There are two very specific and measurable reasons to invest time and money in employee engagement:

1. Employee engagement results in enhanced performance in these areas:
   - Retention
   - Morale

- Being an advocate of the company's products and services
- Bottom line business success
- More dedicated performance

2. Numbers prove it has a *significant link* to profitability

Let's see how it works in the real world. A very large call center, with several hundred employees, boasts 17% turnover in a business that typically averages 80 to 90%. Check out the book *Why Is Everyone Smiling? The Secret Behind Passion, Productivity, and Profit* by Paul Spiegelman, to discover how this call center's engagement approach – including the CEO in a matador's costume – contributes to their phenomenal success.

On the flip side, here's what happens when employees feel disengaged through mistreatment, lack of guidance or just plain ill will: When a customer at a restaurant complained about the restaurant's frequent problem of not having items advertised, the server sat down in the booth with the customer and volunteered negative comments in support of the complaint. Even worse, the server said, "I could sure teach these people something about service and marketing."

Now that's the reason to engage employees.

You're Young, You're Energetic, You're a Creative Thinker

More young people are in management positions today bringing with them fresh energy and new perspectives. These are valuable traits, indispensable to growth and priceless to innovative thinking. They are also traits that can pose challenges to a young manager.

Chances are you are (or will be) managing people who are older than you. Whether they represent Gen X, Gen Jones or Baby Boomer cultures, the need for engagement holds true. In fact, you'll be more successful if you take advantage of each generation's level of "love" for your company.

Despite your accomplishments, workers from other decades may be skeptical, and even critical, of your leadership methods and lack of workforce experience. So how do you become solidly and favorably rooted in the culture (within your department and/or company)? By facing these challenges:

- People require differences in leadership styles. Accept and praise the differences.
- Gen X members may feel competitive with you for leadership jobs (after all, they are the ones closest to you in age and experience at work). Be patient in your desire for advanced positions; and perhaps even ask a Gen Xer to mentor you. You'll gain respect and learn a lot.
- You are probably participatory. Baby Boomers are more hierarchical with power concentrated in senior management. Leave room for each need, altering your style to allow different activities for practice.
- Just as in any multi-cultural situation, meet people where they are. Be prepared to use different management styles with different groups. You may find it helpful to read one of these books: *Communicating for Managerial Effectiveness* or *Managing the Generation Mix: From Collision to Collaboration.*
- No matter who you're dealing with, every employee needs to understand your expectations and provide specific feedback. Be earnest in promoting two-way feedback. Hold meetings where people can express their opinions. Encourage dialogue and demonstrate that you value everyone's input.

Recognize that the elements of interest and concern tend to be different by age group. Many job seekers consider these factors when they are applying for jobs. They want to be certain the company they're considering is a *good citizen* and they won't accept an offer if the company ignores important issues.

- **Environmental concerns**: These are of special interest to younger workers; after all, they're the ones who will inherit the earth. They tend to be informed about things such as carbon footprints, recycling and endangered species. Here's an example: A well known company that makes outdoor gear has now developed a jacket that's made from discarded plastic. So, provide opportunities for younger groups to recycle, time off to participate in environmental activities, and/or develop policies or products that support green initiatives.

Try to influence company leaders to "go green" when they consider projects such as remodeling meeting rooms. One suggestion is to install lighting that automatically goes on when people enter the room and off when they leave.

- **Community involvement**: This factor is important to groups across the board. For your department/group, offer different activities and fundraising jobs that will suit a diverse group. These might include Habitat for Humanity, Save the Whales, the Susan G. Komen Race for the Cure or St. Jude Children's Research Hospital, or restoration of historical institutions.

Work Harder to Gain Respect

There's a possibility that your older employees have *children your age*. As you might suspect, they may have trouble seeing you *as a boss*. You'll have to work harder to define your role and develop a smooth management style. You may have to work extremely diligently to earn respect.

Think of your leadership role as an on-going job interview. You may have heard that the more you allow the interviewer to talk, the more likely you are to get the job. Try this: Give older employees a chance to talk about their projects, any issues they face, concerns they have and so on. Keep quiet. Before you know it, the employee will begin to "give you the job."

Show respect by avoiding the assumption that older workers are ready to be put out to pasture. Many people are working longer than in the past. Plus, they have extensive knowledge and experience. They can be an invaluable asset because they have irreplaceable experience. Enable these employees to mentor and coach younger workers.

Overcome Intimidation

Older workers may fear what will happen when a youthful boss comes on the scene. They may use intimidation as a defense and to gain superiority and power over you. When you join the team, take each team member aside and chat with them individually. Let each one know that you value their input. If you notice that an older worker resists tools that will make them fit in with the younger generation, explain that it's a real time-saver and makes work easier. Offer to have someone coach them. Explain that things change so fast it's hard to keep up, but if they get the basics right they'll find it helpful.

Be Taken Seriously

Put aside defensiveness, power plays, gossiping, bringing personal problems to work, emotional outbursts and favoritism. If workers spot you exhibiting behaviors you wouldn't tolerate in them, they'll quickly decide you're not mature enough to handle a leadership role.

What's the Answer?

Does it seem overwhelming? We've talked about engagement, but that's not the whole story. We have a formula that will guide you in developing teamwork, mutual support, creativity, energy and outstanding contributions on the job among dissimilar employees and is outlined in my book *Light Their Fire: Using Internal Marketing to Ignite Employee Performance and Wow Your Customers.*

We call it the 4 Es:

- **Engage:** Inspire employees to contribute enthusiastically and to "love" their jobs, their managers and their company.

- **Enable:** A business owner we know says, "You can do anything if you have the right tools." The converse is true, too. Tools can include tangible elements such as technological items or proper work chairs. But they also include less obvious support, such as: proper orientation, training, and job aids.

- **Empower:** Verbally support risk taking. Many employees don't understand what empowerment means. Give examples of what you mean and demonstrate the action. Use role plays to show employees how it plays out. Praise risk taking and rally around ideas that don't turn out so favorably. It's like brainstorming: never judge an idea, even if it sounds ridiculous. Even when an idea is un-doable, thank the person(s) who offered it.

- **Ensure:** Work with employees to determine what success looks like and how it can be measured. Set goals and offer guidance on how to meet them. Include discussion of both company results and departmental results. Talk about how they feel about the type of measurement and gain their agreement on the effectiveness of the tools. Plan regular touch point meetings to discuss progress, encourage ongoing success and define course corrections if necessary.

Where Do You Start?

Do you know where you stand in this arena? If not, there are several sure-fire ways to know how you fare. Let's start with some top-line, typical measurements and progress to more in-depth and important methods.

1. Employee Surveys: If your company conducts these, it's a nice way to see general feedback on how you and your company are faring in these four areas. Meet with your team individually and jointly to discuss how you can work together to enable necessary changes identified in the survey. Don't stress the negative information; instead, be positive about solutions. Be cognizant of employees' tendency to clam up or feel put on the spot. Repeated examples of this exercise will increase employees' trust and willingness to participate.

2. Manager Meetings: Invite employees to update meetings to share information about your department and the company as a whole. Host special speakers who can shed light on topical issues.

3. Individual Sessions: Schedule one-on-one meetings with your team members. Talk about their goals for their career, and suggestions they may have for improving processes.

4. Self Evaluation: Some companies require 360-degree evaluations of managers. This means the manager selects a variety of friends, colleagues, employees, vendors and others who can contribute information on the manager's effectiveness. This feedback is anonymous to protect relationships. We've been asked to participate in these where too few people offer information. It can be simple for the manager to figure out who said what. You may prefer to ask for feedback from a mentor. Also, read management books and compare their advice with how you really act. It's time for an honest reality check!

Help! When Will I Do My Own Work?

Are you feeling overwhelmed? Wondering how you'll find the time to do all this and still meet your own boss's expectations?

Remember that magic wand we talked about? There is no quick way to become a trusted leader – someone who can engage employees with the flick of a switch. The good news is that if you're making a genuine effort, people will see it. You can't fake any element of the 4 Es. It doesn't take long for employees to see through a mask.

When you think that it's not possible to accomplish all this AND do your job, consider this: Engaged team members contribute more, avoid dragging the team down (which saves you time), and make it easier for you to delegate with confidence. They'll do a lot of your day-to-day job for you, which is one element of what good management and leadership is about. And, best of all, they'll make it a joy for you to come to work.

About Sara Roberts:

Sara Roberts is the President & CEO of Roberts Golden Consulting (RobertsGolden.com), a consultancy based in San Francisco, CA. Her company focuses on providing change management and employee engagement solutions for a wide variety of Fortune 500 companies. She is also co-author of the best-selling book, *Light Their Fire: Using Internal Marketing to Ignite Employee Performance and Wow Your Customers.*

PART FOUR

All About Lisa

"I truly understand and respect your Millennial mindset.
So I know you like to do things your way...I simply ask that
you do things *the right way*! Your generation has witnessed,
first hand, corruption at historic levels, the deterioration
of trust in leaders in the public and private sectors, and
employee dissatisfaction on the rise. So take those lessons with
you into every level of leadership you reach, and *choose* to
make a difference!"

~ Lisa Orrell, Author of this book, 20-year business owner, and a Mom (whose
young son will be looking to your generation as his future role models)

CHAPTER SIXTEEN

How Lisa Can Help You: Coaching, Assessment Tools & Resources

LEADERSHIP & CAREER COACHING:

I'm a Leadership & Career Coach for Millennials who value personal growth, want to excel in their careers, accelerate their path to professional and personal fulfillment…and for those who understand the benefits of working with a personal coach to help make it happen. And if you don't understand the "benefits" yet, just being open to coaching means you're on the right path!

A majority of respected senior executives, C-level professionals, world leaders, premier athletes, and successful entrepreneurs, hired personal coaches early on, and continue to hire coaches now, for a variety of reasons. Why? They benefit from it.

Some people are confused about what professional coaching is and is not. Coaching is <u>not</u> therapy, counseling or psychotherapy. My role as your personal Leadership & Career Coach is to be your guide and partner, and utilize my skills, knowledge, experience, and professional coach training to help you exceed your own expectations.

There are a wide variety of coaches: Life Coaches, Executive Coaches, Financial Coaches, Small Business Coaches, Leadership Coaches, Relationship Coaches, Career Coaches, etc. <u>But regardless of a coach's niche, we all have 2 things in common</u>:

We work with people who are already in a healthy place in their lives, but that want to continue growing and excelling – personally and/or professionally.

And "Life Coaching" is a component of ANY type of coaching. It's all about YOU and YOUR life, so how couldn't it be?

My Purpose As Your Leadership & Career Coach Is To:
- Help you *uncover* your goals, roadblocks, opportunities, and vision
- Build and/or maintain *your confidence* to achieve your goals
- Create a plan to help *you achieve* your short-term & long-term goals faster
- Provide effective feedback that *supports* your goals, objectives and vision
- Provide you with a *safe and confidential* space to be open, grow, share & learn
- Assist you with *making decisions*, keep you on track, evaluate your choices & give you clarity
- Bring out *your strengths* and overcome your weaknesses
- Not be a "yes" woman, but provide you with *honest feedback and insights*
- *Remain objective* & approach our relationship without judgment, criticism or bias
- Help you become the exceptional leader, and person, *you envision*
- Be *your sounding board* when faced with challenges at work (or in your personal life), and provide you with effective feedback

- Make sure both of us *have a lot of fun* throughout the process!

To learn more about my coaching process and how I can benefit you, visit my website. *There's an entire Coaching Section that can answer many of your questions:* **TheOrrellGroup.com.**

ONLINE, CONFIDENTIAL, ASSESSMENT TOOLS:

Assessing your skills and personality traits to better understand yourself is critical to your success. And chances are, if you work for a company with Leadership and Management Training Programs, you have taken, or will take, assessments. But many companies don't offer formal training *of any kind* when it comes to leadership or management, so I suggest that you go to my website to check out some online tools you can take on your own.

Go to TheOrrellGroup.com and click on *Products*. You will see a variety of online assessment tools that will: Assess and improve your leadership effectiveness; help you assess why you get along with some people but not with others; determine and assess your personal management style; give you insights into your management competency; determine your strengths and unveil weaknesses (you maybe weren't aware of!); and that will assess your *emotional* intelligence (your ability to connect, or disconnect, with others personally and professionally).

You can take one assessment or all of them! They are very inexpensive (some under $20), and each one only takes around 5-15 minutes to complete. Plus, *all results are private & confidential*, AND each one provides you with a detailed report of the findings, what they mean, and how you can use the info.

They are actually really fun to do, easy to complete, and will provide you with useful info that will benefit your life and career.

RESOURCES:

Here is a short list of business books you should consider reading. They can all help you become the young, respected and effective leader you aspire to be:

1. *The 21 Irrefutable Laws of Leadership*, by John C. Maxwell

2. *The 360° Leader: Developing Your Influence from Anywhere in the Organization*, by John C. Maxwell

3. *Leading From The Heart: Choosing to be a Servant Leader*, by Jack Kahl

4. *Make Their Day! Employee Recognition That Works*, by Cindy Ventrice

5. *Me 2.0: Build A Powerful Brand to Achieve Career Success*, by Dan Schawbel

6. *The Heart of a Leader: Insights on the Art of Influence,* by Ken Blanchard

7. *1001 Ways to Reward Employees, by Bob Nelson PH.D.*

SEMINARS & WORKSHOPS BY LISA: Contact Lisa or visit her website for up-dates. She adds new topics regularly!

SEMINARS (These can also be presented as Webinars):

1. Get A Grip on Gen Y: Insights and Strategies for Effectively Attracting, Recruiting & Retaining the Millennial Generation *(for HR, internal recruiters, and executives)*

2. Get A Grip On Leadership: Preparing Millennials to Be Effective, Respected, Young Leaders at Work *(for your Millennial employees)*

3. Managing Millennials Seminar: How to Recruit, Manage, Motivate and Retain Our New (Unique!) Generation of Young Professionals *(for anyone managing Millennial talent)*

4. Global Millennials: Insights Into Our First Global Generation & Their Impact on Employers Worldwide *(for mid-to-senior level executives)*

5. Understanding Generations for Sales Acceleration *(for sales teams)*

6. Improving Communication Across the Generations *(for all employees)*

WORKSHOPS/PROGRAMS:

1. Millennial Business Boot Camp *(full-day workshop for your Millennial employees)*

2. Transitioning to Leadership Program: How to Effectively Move Your Millennial Employees Into Leadership Roles *(co-facilitated with Camille Smith, President of Work In Progress Coaching, Inc., 25-year Executive & Leadership Coach)*

CONTACT LISA:

Contact Lisa today to be your *personal* Leadership & Career Coach, or to conduct a seminar, workshop, keynote, or leadership-coaching program for your company, school, or professional association!

Lisa Orrell, CPC
The Generation Relations Expert
Speaker • Author • Leadership & Career Coach For Millennials
www.TheOrrellGroup.com
Lisa@TheOrrellGroup.com
1-888-254-LISA

Check out Lisa's Busy Blog: Blog.GenerationRelations.com

Listen to Lisa's Popular Podcast:
MillennialsInMotion.podomatic.com

Follow Lisa on Twitter @GenerationsGuru

Join Lisa On: FaceBook, MySpace and LinkedIn

ABOUT THE AUTHOR

Lisa Orrell, CPC
The Generation Relations Expert
Speaker • Author • Leadership & Career Coach for Millennials

Lisa started her first advertising agency in Silicon Valley when she was just 25 years old and ran her award-winning agency for two decades. And as a 20+ year business owner and marketing expert (with vast management and leadership experience), Lisa has always researched the "next big trends" that affect business and workforce environments.

Spotting the trend of shifting dynamics in the multigenerational workforce several years ago, Lisa began researching the impact of Millennials entering the professional landscape. This led to writing and publishing her first book in 2007: *Millennials Incorporated: The Big Business of Recruiting, Managing and Retaining The World's New Generation of Young Professionals.* This book was named a finalist in *ForeWord Magazine's* prestigious "Book of the Year" competition.

Professionally, she is now known as The Generation Relations Expert, and is an in-demand speaker who conducts a variety of dynamic seminars, workshops and keynotes that: Improve generation relations at work; improve the recruitment, management and retention of Millennial talent; and that motivate & empower Millennials to be effective young leaders in the workforce.

In addition to speaking, Lisa is also a professional Leadership & Career Coach for Millennials who are aspiring to enter, or currently in, leadership roles at work. She has received her Professional Coach training through an intensive certification program accredited by the International Coach Federation.

And based on her expert status, Lisa has been featured on ABC, MSNBC and NPR, and her expert commentary and articles have appeared in countless national and international media, such as (partial list): *The New York Times, Wall Street Journal, U.S. News & World Report, Human Resource Executive, Recruitment & Retention*, HR.com, FoxBusiness.com, BNET.com, Monster.com, CareerBuilder.com, *ComputerWorld*, Universum's *Trainee Guides* for Norway, Sweden and Denmark, China's *HerWorld* magazine, *Diversity Business, Latino University* magazine, *Black Enterprise*, Magna Publications for Colleges, *Northwestern Business Review*, and *Employee Benefit News*.

Lisa is a graduate of San Jose State University, and resides in San Jose, CA with her long time partner, Adrienne, and their young son, Jenner.

Hi Bubba! The book is done...let's play! Mama loves you lots.

LaVergne, TN USA
11 February 2010
172648LV00008B/30/P